ASSESSING WHAT PROFESSORS DO

Recent Titles in
Contributions to the Study of Education

Assessing What Professors Do

AN INTRODUCTION TO ACADEMIC PERFORMANCE APPRAISAL IN HIGHER EDUCATION

David A. Dilts, Lawrence J. Haber, and Donna Bialik

Contributions to the Study of Education, Number 61

GREENWOOD PRESS
Westport, Connecticut • London

Library of Congress Cataloging-in-Publication Data

Dilts, David A.
    Assessing what professors do : an introduction to academic
performance appraisal in higher education / David A. Dilts, Lawrence
J. Haber, and Donna Bialik.
      p. cm.—(Contributions to the study of education, ISSN
0196–707X ; no. 61)
    Includes bibliographical references and index.
    ISBN 0–313–26761–8 (alk. paper)
    1. College teachers—United States—Rating of. I. Haber,
Lawrence J. II. Bialik, Donna. III. Title. IV. Series.
LB2333.D55   1994
378.1'22—dc20   93–30978

British Library Cataloguing in Publication Data is available.

Library of Congress Catalog Card Number: 93–30978
ISBN: 0–313–26761–8
ISSN: 0196–707X

First published in 1994

Greenwood Press, 88 Post Road West, Westport, CT 06881
An imprint of Greenwood Publishing Group, Inc.   .

Printed in the United States of America

∞™
The paper used in this book complies with the
Permanent Paper Standard issued by the National
Information Standards Organization (Z39.48–1984).

10 9 8 7 6 5 4 3 2 1

Contents

Preface

This book is written for the academician, administrator and anyone else interested in faculty performance appraisal or evaluation in higher education. While there has been a significant amount written concerning the evaluation of faculty performance, there has been little attempt to integrate issues of ethics in the appraisal literature. The fundamental purpose of this book is to examine faculty performance appraisal. However, the authors' approach is to also integrate discussions of ethical and legal obligations into the presentation.

The examination of faculty performance appraisal is a controversial topic. Much of what has been written and much of what is known has come from the perspective of scholars in education. The authors of this book are economists writing from the perspective of economists concerned with education and faculty performance. Rigorous economic models have been avoided to make the text accessible to all who might benefit. Further, the authors are faculty members in a school of business, and the orientation of the book is focused on business and social science programs. This is not to say that the authors support the notion that universities should emulate business practices in personnel or service delivery decisions. In fact, academic decision making should not and cannot be constrained by profit-maximizing goals if educational progress is the goal. However, certain economic and business perspectives provide useful insights for the practice of faculty performance appraisals. As such, it is believed that this book will be a useful guide to novice administrators and/or faculty members faced with the task of helping to create or attempting to survive an ethical evaluation program for their academic units. It reports on much of the literature on evaluation, but is primarily a pragmatic guide to evaluation.

The main text of this book is organized in three parts. Part I contains three chapters concerned with the structure and ethics of evaluation. A comparison of performance and non-performance based personnel decisions is offered, after which the basic procedures followed in personnel evaluation are examined. These procedures provide a frame of reference for the following two chapters that deal with criteria used in performance appraisals and rules of evidence used in those appraisals.

Part II begins with a discussion of general considerations in the establishment of the appropriate mix of professorial activities (i.e., teaching, research and service) to be evaluated. What follows is a review of many of the specific criteria reported in the literature used to evaluate faculty performance in teaching, in research and in service. Due attention is also paid to the interrelations among these areas.

Part III offers a discussion of the environmental influences on faculty performance appraisal. In particular, the effects of the legal system and of unionization and collective bargaining upon professorial performance appraisal at universities in the United States are examined.

In an appendix, the book contains the policy statements of the American Association of University Professors (AAUP) relevant to personnel evaluation. Finally, there is an annotated bibliography of selected references concerning faculty performance appraisal.

There are many persons who have contributed significantly to this project and who deserve a public statement of our gratitude. Linda Haber did a great deal of proofreading and made many useful comments. Clarence R. Deitsch suggested several improvements. Penny Herber typed several pages of this manuscript and was always willing to help. The editors at Greenwood Press were patient as this project evolved, changed directions and took final form, and they were tolerant of several delays. Phil Saunders, Yar Ebadi and John Manzer were invaluable resources from whom we learned much, and their contributions to our understanding are most certainly reflected in the pages of this book.

Finally, there are several persons with whom we work at Indiana-Purdue University at Fort Wayne whose views of appropriate academic appraisal piqued our interest and resulted in this project being undertaken. Naturally, any errors of omission or commission are the responsibility of the authors, even though Larry Haber drove the other two authors beyond distraction in seeking out the most trivial style and grammatical points with which to take issue (the Preface was written while Larry was on leave in Iowa).

Part I

Ethics and the
Performance Appraisal System

Chapter 1

An Introduction to Faculty Performance Appraisal

PERFORMANCE VERSUS NONPERFORMANCE BASED DECISION MAKING

The subject matter with which this book deals is performance appraisal. As such, the focus will be on topics concerned with faculty performance and its evaluation. This does not mean, however, that many of the decisions that are discussed here will not be made using nonperformance based criteria or, at least, be heavily influenced by factors other than professional performance. It also does not mean that performance based decisions are the only way with which to deal with personnel matters.

The first decision that must be made by faculty and/or administration is what type of system will be used in their organization; or whether a mix of performance and nonperformance based decisions will be made. As will be discussed later in this chapter and in more detail in Chapter 2, performance based appraisal systems are an important factor in increasing the overall effectiveness of an academic organization. The motivational aspects of performance based systems can be an exceedingly important tool in accomplishing the objectives of a university. However, there are arguments in support of nonperformance based systems. For example, salary decisions that permit a portion of the available resources to be distributed as a cost-of-living adjustment are not current performance based. If distributed as a percentage increase based on current salary, the cost-of-living adjustment certainly recognizes (in part) past performance, but maintaining the purchasing power of current salaries may be of substantial concern to the faculty and administration.

In large measure, whether a performance or nonperformance based appraisal system is adopted is a matter of policy to be determined by each academic organization. The circumstances facing an institution, the variations that exist in productivity, the internal labor markets facing the school, and the organizational culture are the internal factors that will determine which type of decision-making criteria best serves the institution. There are also several environmental influences that will be important determinants of the type of system adopted. Among these are external law for state schools, such as legislative enactment of budgets, school missions and clientele to be served. Alumni, the potential employers of students, benefactors, and the general public may also influence the culture of the organization and may have specific demands that will affect the type of appraisal system adopted by the organization.

PERFORMANCE APPRAISAL

There are few issues in higher education that elicit as much controversy as faculty performance appraisal.[1] Self-interest, campus politics and conflicting evidence often cloud the understanding of the goals and processes that combine to make a fair and effective performance appraisal system. Even so, the effectiveness and the fairness of the evaluation system used by an academic institution will do much to shape the culture and the quality of the academic outputs of that organization.[2] In short, there may be no more important policy constructed and implemented within the academic organization than the performance assessment policy.[3]

Faculty performance appraisal (assessment and evaluation are also used as synonyms for appraisal throughout this book) is generally identified as a system of activities with specific individual and often organizational goals, identified rewards and sometimes punishments for individuals, substantive criteria upon which to determine whether goals have been attained, and procedures whereby evidence is gathered to which criteria will be applied to reach specific decisions. The practices that have evolved in colleges and universities concerning the appraisal of faculty performance vary substantially across the academic landscape. They vary from unwritten understandings (or sometimes individual administrators' views) concerning personnel decisions to lengthy, legalistic documents specifying virtually every aspect of the conduct of the performance appraisal system. This observation is simultaneously the major strength and the worst weakness of faculty performance appraisal as practiced in U.S. colleges and universities.

The strength arises from the fact that faculty performance appraisal must be tailored to the specific needs and missions of the institution for it to serve both the organization and individual faculty members. There is no single system of performance appraisal that has gained universal acceptance, which suggests that universities *have* attempted to tailor their systems.

The weakness arises from the fact that the flexibility to serve the collective needs of the faculty and the organization may occasionally allow, though rarely, performance appraisal to be perverted to serve individual purposes or the selfish interests of an individual, often to the detriment of students, other faculty members, academic quality or organizational goals. In other words, the democratic processes that are typical of most universities contain all the grand ideals and, at least the potential of, all the evils of the dark side of any democracy.

THE STRUCTURE OF APPRAISAL SYSTEMS

Faculty performance appraisal systems rarely, if ever, exist in a vacuum. Faculty performance appraisal is used in a complex variety of decisions concerning both individual faculty members and the organization. Because of the complex applications of faculty performance evaluation, the appropriate beginning point for any discussion of assessment must be the structure or procedures involved with performance assessment.

Appraisal mechanisms are not ends, but they are means by which an academic organization measures success, identifies problem areas, and monitors progress. In other words, appraisal systems are supporting mechanisms for the delivery of academic outputs. As supporting mechanisms, appraisal systems must be designed in such a way as to facilitate organizational activities.

Performance assessment systems serve three functions within the university. These are: to identify and evaluate the performance of individual faculty members, to provide incentives for faculty members, and to monitor the progress of the institution toward attaining its goals and objectives. With individual performance assessment, it is not uncommon for universities to have separate procedures for salary increase decisions, promotion and tenure and for retention decisions. Even in such cases, it is typical that much of the information relied upon for each decision concerning individual personnel matters is the same evidence. Frequently, universities establish the procedures for individual faculty performance appraisal separately from the mechanisms used to monitor organizational performance. It is also common for the information needed for the monitoring of organizational performance to be that which is gathered in individual performance appraisal.

The authors suggest that a unified appraisal system increases the efficiency of the total assessment process. With modern information system technology it is a relatively simple task to create, maintain and update a data base from which current productivity reports can be generated for individual faculty members, departments, schools or even the entire university. The question becomes one of centralization and uniform reporting mechanisms that are sufficiently flexible to permit accounting for the individual missions of the various units of the university and for individual academic freedom within the missions of the university.

The information necessary for year-end salary decisions is frequently exactly the same information needed in making retention decisions. Retention decisions typically rely on the same information that is necessary for promotion and tenure decisions. Therefore, rather than to create committees and use substantial amounts of faculty resources in gathering and regathering the same sorts of information, common sense dictates that a single pass is a far more efficient use of both administrative and faculty assets.

Several programs and most universities are periodically subjected to external reviews for accreditation purposes. The benefits of a unified data-gathering system are obvious in such situations. Further, strategic planning is (or should be) an integral part of the administration of any academic organization. The monitoring of the progress toward attaining the goals of the strategic plan requires the gathering of data upon which the planning and revising process depends. Again, the benefits of a unified approach suggested here are obvious.[4]

Performance appraisal systems specify criteria for judging performance. The criteria are generally based on the mission of the academic organization and are typically applied to evidence by an evaluating authority. There is significant variation in the evidence that is typically required by academic organizations, and the quantum of evidence depends not only on the purpose of the decision, but on the institution's mission. The evidence is generally gathered by a committee or an administrator with the participation of faculty member(s). The evidence is then initially weighed by either an administrator or a committee. It is also common that there is administrative and/or committee review of the initial decision and the evidence upon which it was based, and frequently there are successive reviews at each organizational level (department, school, university). The

Table 1
Procedure for Promotion and Tenure Decisions

Step	Organizational Level	Activity	Reports To
1	Individual Faculty Member	Gathers Information	Department P & T Committee
2	Department P & T Committee	Weighs Evidence, Applies Criteria, and Makes Recommendation	Department Chair
3	Department Chair	Weighs Evidence, Applies Criteria, and Makes Recommendation	College Committee
4	College Committee	Reviews Lower Level Decision and Makes Recommendation	College Dean
5	College Dean	Reviews Lower Level Decision and Makes Recommendation	Vice President for Faculty
6	Vice President for Faculty Affairs	Reviews Lower Level Decision and Makes Recommendation	University President
7	President of University	Reviews Lower Level Decision and Makes Recommendation	Board of Trustees or Regents
8	Board of Trustees or Regents	Makes Final Decision and Informs Candidate	Individual Faculty Member
9	Individual Faculty Member	Accepts or Appeals, if Appeal	Faculty Grievance Review Board (Decision Leaves P & T Process)

evaluating authorities, the evidence to be examined, the methods to gather evidence and how decisions are to be made are procedural issues. Frequently these procedural issues will be formalized with respect to specific decisions to be made, such as salary determinations, retention, tenure, promotion, reductions in force and resource allocations. It is not uncommon, across universities, for each of these appraisal procedures to be specified in a separate policy with differing structures.

Often, appraisal systems will specify other activities designed to assure fairness and due process. For example, grievance procedures or appeal processes will normally be constructed as a portion of an appraisal system or identified as an adjunct to the assessment process.

Table 1 shows the typical procedure used in promotion and tenure cases. There are numerous variations on the process contained in Table 1. Occasionally there will be a university level committee; sometimes there is no school or college level committee. In some institutions, the faculty of the department serve as the department's promotion and tenure com-

mittee and the chairperson may or may not have responsibilities beyond
a faculty member, except for service in the department's deliberations and
recommendations. Occasionally in unionized facilities there is no formal
role for the faculty but informal input into the administration's decision
making.

Retention decisions for untenured or term faculty members frequently
follow the process specified for promotion and tenure decisions specified
in Table 1. Salary decisions and sabbatical leaves (and other resource
allocation matters) will generally follow procedures similar to those in
Table 1. What is of interest is that, too often, each category of decision
will have its own procedural framework. While the decisions to be made
differ, and the criteria may be different, there is simply no compelling
reason for the procedures to significantly differ. The procedure shown in
Table 1 is a multiple-step process in which the basic decision making is
done at the lower levels where the most specific criteria and discipline
specific expertise are to be found. The higher authorities serve in a review
capacity to assure that lower levels did not miss something and that the
decisions were based on sound evidence and/or reasoning. There may also
be significant differences in the composition of committees and how
membership is determined. At some schools, Kansas State's College of
Business is one, the department committees are those members of the
faculty holding the status for which the candidate has applied. At Indiana
University in Fort Wayne, the committees are elected by the voting faculty
at the school and department levels, but the chancellor appoints campus
committee members.

Another way to look at this type of structure is that the dean and college
committees serve a leveling function for the college, to assure that basic
fairness and perhaps minimum levels of performance are attained across
the college. The next successive organizational levels perform the same
type of function to assure that fairness and minimum performance levels
are attained across the university.

The argument for uniform procedures and evidence gathering is rather
simple and straightforward. Retention decisions (except for term faculty
members) are (or should be) predictive of whether someone is making
adequate progress toward tenure. Promotion decisions are, in many cases,
directly tied to tenure, but if not directly connected do involve similar
criteria and evidence at most schools. If salary and other resource allocation decisions are performance based (most are at least in part), the
performance basis for promotion and tenure decisions should not
significantly differ because salaries are probably the most meaningful
signal to an individual of the value of his or her services to the institution.

The independent gathering and weighing of information, the multiple reconsideration of candidates' cases, and the variations that may occur in the decision-making process are strong arguments for a unified procedure. The arguments against a unified procedure include the centralization of decision-making authority and the increased costs in time and effort for fewer faculty members who serve on the unified committee. In large measure the cultural and political values held on the campus will do much to direct whether a unified system is possible, but it is clear that there are significant efficiency gains to be made from the adoption of such a system. It is also clear that there will be greater consistency across the various personnel decisions in any given academic year. Consistency across time depends more on the criteria and the dynamics of the university and school missions.

It may also be effectively argued that eight or nine steps in the process are simply excessive. The most efficient system would be for the department committee to make recommendations to the chairperson, who in turn makes a recommendation to the dean, who in turn recommends to the president the appropriate decision. The simple, four-step process is far less cumbersome and therefore more economically efficient. However, concern for fairness and for the leveling of decision has caused many academic organizations to proliferate steps in the decision-making process.

ETHICS AND APPRAISAL

Throughout this book, references will be made to ethics or widely accepted standards of conduct in academe. The effectiveness of the procedures and criteria and the weighing of evidence critically depend on the ethics of decision makers. No matter how well policies are constructed, they will be no more effective than the people who administer them. Alternatively, even bad policy can sometimes be made serviceable if the people charged with its implementation are ethical and capable. It is a relatively easy matter to present the current status of research and procedures, and to discuss the aspects of performance appraisal. Positive analysis is generally easier than normative analysis.

The conduct of decision makers within the framework of appraisal procedures and criteria in weighing the evidence is normative analysis. Ethics is the study of how people should behave in their specific roles. A caveat is therefore in order. Even though there has been substantial discussion of academic ethics in the literature, there is little agreement on the need for a code of ethics for college professors in general, and there even exists some disagreement as to what such a code should specify.

Rather than impose, totally, what the authors view as appropriate ethics, the various policy statements of the AAUP are included as an appendix, simply for quick reference to what that organization has stated as appropriate conduct.

SUMMARY AND CONCLUSIONS

Policies concerning salary, promotion, tenure, and any resource allocation activity are generally subject to either a performance or non-performance based decision-making system. The first step in formulating these policies is to determine whether a performance or nonperformance based system should be adopted. The purpose of this book is to review the former. The latter is simple and needs little further discussion.

Procedure is the structure in which decision making takes place. Most performance based appraisal systems are multiple step processes. The multiple steps in the process generally flow upward through the organization from the individual faculty member's level through the department, school and university. Procedures for performance appraisal facilitate the gathering of evidence concerning performance, establish criteria for the weighing of the evidence and establish a flow of recommendations and information from one academic or administrative level of the organization to another. Most procedures also provide for grievance or appeal authorities after the final decision has been made. These procedures are frequently external to the performance appraisal system.

The gathering of evidence can be made more efficient through the use of a uniform reporting procedure supported by a modern information system. The efficiency gains that are normal to such uniform information systems are obvious. The centralization and potential for constraining the missions of academic units and possibly limiting academic freedom must be recognized when constructing such an information system.

The ethics of those charged with the responsibility of making decisions within the performance appraisal framework are of critical importance. The conduct of faculty members and administrators will, in large measure, determine how effective and fair performance appraisal is within any organization, academic or otherwise.

NOTES

1. Jack C. Soper, "Soft Research on a Hard Subject: Student Evaluations Reconsidered," *Journal of Economic Education* (Fall 1973), pp. 22–26.
2. See M. Sashkin, "Appraising Appraisal: Ten Lessons from Research for

Practice," *Organizational Dynamics* (Winter 1981), pp. 37–50, for further discussion of the interactions of appraisal with culture and across organizational levels.

3. J. J. Siegfried and R. Fels, "Research on Teaching College Economics: A Survey," *Journal of Economic Literature*, vol. 17 (September 1979), pp. 923–69.

4. For example, see Pai-Cheng Chu, "Developing Expert Systems for Human Resource Planning and Management," *Human Resource Planning*, no. 3 (1990), pp. 159–78.

Chapter 2

The Criteria for
Faculty Performance Appraisal

The purpose of this chapter is to examine criteria in academic performance appraisal. A general discussion and definitions of criteria will be offered prior to proceeding to the creation and the role of criteria in performance assessment. Finally, a discussion of the effects of criteria will be offered.

The criteria for decision making in performance appraisal are the standards by which professional performance will be judged. These standards or criteria must be designed such that they provide specific guidance to the decision makers as to the appropriate decision concerning any body of performance evidence before them. The criteria also notify faculty members of what is expected in order to gain tenure, promotion, be retained or to receive a salary increase.

Criteria vary on at least two planes. There are broad (or very general criteria) and narrow criteria (very specific criteria). Broad criteria provide general guidance as to what is expected. At higher organizational levels, general criteria such as excellence in teaching or original contributions in research and creative endeavors are common. This permits academic subunits to create more specific, or narrower, criteria so as to implement their specific portion of the institution's mission.

Criteria may also be subjective or objective. As will be discussed in greater detail below, objective criteria are those that lend themselves to decisions based on quantifiable evidence, without the need for professional opinion to reach a conclusion. Subjective criteria are typically used on evidence that need not be quantified and requires a professional opinion to reach a conclusion.

Procedures are the methods and actions necessary to implement the criteria of an appraisal system. The evidence to which the criteria are to be applied is what operationalizes the criteria. In other words, the criteria are implemented through procedures to translate evidence into decisions concerning professional performance.

CRITERIA: THEIR CREATION AND USE

The creation of criteria and hence the types of evidence to be weighed is a function of the organizational goals and objectives. It is not uncommon for a university to promulgate a general policy statement concerning personnel actions and resource allocations and permit schools and colleges to develop more specific policies that are not in contravention to the university's policy statement. Schools and colleges may then permit departments and other subunits to provide for even more specific policies consistent with the upper-level policy. This structure is analogous to a funnel: broad at the top and more narrow at the bottom. This form of structure provides for a balance to accomplish the university's broad goals, but permits flexibility for diverse academic units to accomplish the narrowing goals of their own subunits. For example, it is doubtful that a tenure policy specifically tailored to a Ph.D.-granting physics department would serve the needs of an undergraduate fine arts department, yet both may exist on the same campus whose major goals include excellence in teaching and research.

Figure 1 summarizes the establishment of decision criteria in performance appraisal. The funneling of goals down the organization from the university level to the departmental level exhibits a direct correlation with the breadth of the appraisal criteria developed and applied at each level.

Procedural issues also mirror what is presented in Figure 1. As the appraisal criteria become more specific, the procedures necessary to implement specific criteria will generally become more specific. The reason for this is that, at the two highest levels in the academic organization, policies will be little more than general policy statements. As one moves down the organization, the more specific goals of the department and other subunits will require more specific evidence concerning performance. The specificity of evidence will require increased specificity in the gathering and weighing of that evidence.

Where most faculty members and administrators become involved in the structural issues of performance appraisal systems is at the departmental or subunit levels. Faculty members and lower-level administrators may

Figure 1
Performance Appraisal Criteria Flow Chart

Organizational Level	Goals and Objectives	Evaluation Criteria
University	Very Broad	General
\		/
School/College	Broad	More Specific
\		/
Department	Narrow	Very Specific
\		/
Individual Faculty Member		

also become involved in the creation and review of higher-level policies as collective bargaining representatives, committee members or faculty senators. To effectively serve in these capacities, the role of each level in the policy-making process must be fully understood. In this respect, each college and university will have developed its own organizational culture. In academic organizations with collective bargaining arrangements, it is common for faculty members to have some input into the union's bargaining committee and the union and administration will determine what will occur at the upper levels. In self-governing institutions, policies are typically a function of democratic processes through a faculty senate or committee system, and the administration's role is to implement the policies established by the faculty. Top-down management systems, while still relatively rare, will sometimes give faculty "meet and confer" rights through a committee, but final decisions as to the goals, assessment criteria, and appraisal procedures may rest solely with the administration. This diversity of organizational structures and cultures makes generalizations, beyond those offered, dangerous.

Again, the structure of the appraisal system is dependent upon institutional goals. However, academic organizations have external influences. Alumni, benefactors, state legislatures, boards of trustees or regents and higher education commissions will often have substantial influence over the institutional goals, and this influence will sometimes be reflected in the criteria adopted for personnel decisions. Often the administration, particularly higher levels, will have greater contact with these external sources of influence than with the faculty and lower-level administrators.

A strong faculty will assure that its voice is heard in establishing goals for the university because of the direct impact of these goals on personnel decisions. Faculty must also be vigilant to assure that the criteria and procedures established at higher levels of the organization permit sufficient lower-level flexibility to allow the department to accomplish its specific goals. Faculty also must perform a watchdog function, in the absence of a union, to assure proper administration of the performance appraisal system. Unfortunately, much of the faculty role described in this paragraph is confounded by campus politics and requires the political skills that are often held in contempt by scholars. Knowledge concerning the proper structuring of the appraisal system is simply not enough; it must also be made possible to enact and administer proper evaluation mechanisms.

Substance and Criteria

The establishment of criteria for performance appraisal is dependent upon the mission of the university and its subunits.[1] However, there are other factors that are of significance in determining the appropriate criteria for performance appraisal. It is important to remember that not only does the performance appraisal system monitor the performance of individuals, it also provides a basis for judgments concerning the effectiveness of the total organization. The distinction is important because criteria for individual faculty member performance must support the criteria used to judge the overall effectiveness of the organization. For example, a university may specify excellence in teaching as a broad goal. The college may specify that course material be current, classes be well-received and enrollments increased as its goal. For a department to specify that only student evaluation questionnaire results are required for individual performance appraisals fails to support two out of three of the college's goals. Every individual may be evaluated as an excellent teacher, but the department failed to support the currency and enrollment goals. However, an individual instructor may not be able to influence enrollments, but certainly the professor is the one who determines the currency of the courses she/he teaches. If productivity and quality are to be fostered at the organizational level, the individual appraisal must be well connected to the aggregate goals and objectives.[2]

In the private sector, criteria for performance appraisal are routinely generated from a job analysis.[3] As will be discussed in Chapter 4, the law also requires that criteria for individual employee appraisals must be based in what is actually required of the employee, and hence must be founded upon a valid job analysis if legal problems are to be avoided. Potential legal problems should be sufficient cause for most organizations to implement job analyses; however, the substantive nature of any performance criteria generates the utility of performance appraisal. No performance appraisal system will be any more valuable than the criteria it applies. No criteria are of value unless they specifically apply to the substantive behaviors and/or outputs of the job that is to be performed.

Probably the most objective of all performance criteria is seniority. It is a relatively simple task to determine how long someone has been on the job. That is why seniority is so commonly specified as the criterion for retention, recall, promotion and pay raises in union contracts. However, seniority suffers from being unable to substantively differentiate between various levels of performance (either quantity or quality). For positions where there is little variation in performance, seniority may be an adequate criterion. However, for professional employees, particularly in positions where there is a recognized large variation in the quantity or quality of outputs, substantive aspects of the performance should be measured and substantive criteria employed to assure levels of productivity necessary to accomplish organizational goals. In other words, to determine what an appropriate criterion is, a job analysis should be performed to answer the question, "What do professors do?"

What do professors do? That is the central question this book seeks to answer. Even with this question, there are differences in the missions of universities, schools and departments that will cause significant variations in the answers to this question. Criteria adopted for performance appraisal must be substantive where the academic goals are substantive. If professors are expected to meet classes, have office hours and attend committee meetings, little more than a time clock and an attendance sheet is required to determine the professor's location at specific times of the day. If more is contemplated, then the criteria become more complex.

APPRAISAL, EDUCATION AND MOTIVATION

From the perspective of economists, education is simply the acquisition of human capital by students. The professor's role is to direct, instruct, facilitate, test and encourage (among other things), but it is the student who acquires skills, knowledge and abilities. Scholars in the fields in education offer more precise (and useful) definitions of education, but for present purposes the acquisition of human capital definition is sufficient. Educational outputs are the development of students' human capital. The typical professor's role in this process is the discovery (or creation) of knowledge, instruction in the given discipline and service to the university and profession to assure that these activities continue. The inputs of the educational process are also elements of human capital possessed by the faculty who are teaching, researching and doing service activities. Unlike a goods-producing industry, educational outputs cannot be physically gauged, weighed or inspected for defects. In the absence of a physical product, assessment of quantity and quality of output becomes more complicated. Education, while it may have certain tangible correlates, is more closely associated with the service industries than with goods-producing industries. The intangible characteristics of service (education included) require far more sophistication in performance appraisal because of the identification and measurement problems associated with the assessment of performance without a tangible output.

The identification problem is, again, a simple restatement of the title of this book, "What do professors do?" Research articles are tangible, their quality or influence in the profession may not be; do professors publish or do they seek truth? Students may find jobs and get admitted to graduate school; did we help or simply delay their progress? Unless the desired outputs are identified they cannot be measured.

Tangible outputs can be counted or tested for tensile strength, but how do we measure the progress a student has made in a curriculum? Testing can provide some answers, so can student evaluations, but these are imperfect measurement devices. The validity and reliability of the measures chosen to appraise performance will determine the utility of the appraisal system.[4]

These matters of identification and measurement are important to the structure and administration of an appropriate appraisal system. However, the appraisal system will also affect professorial behaviors.[5] Rewards and punishments are generally connected to any decision that is made using an appraisal system. Promotion to associate professor is a reward, and if it carries a stipend it is two rewards for performance. A denial of tenure is a punishment. Whether a person reacts to the appraisal system and its inherent rewards and punishments depends on whether that person is extrinsically or intrinsically motivated, and the relative strengths of those motivations.

In the simple case where someone is purely extrinsically motivated, the person's behavior will be in response to external stimuli. If a person is purely intrinsically motivated, his behaviors are responses to his own (internal) value systems. In reality, most people have behavioral responses, in different situations and with a variety of issues, that can be classified as intrinsic in one endeavor and extrinsic in another arena. In some cases, both forms of motivation are present, and the relative strength of their value systems with respect to the external stimuli will determine their behaviors. This is true of professionals, blue collar workers, and even criminals.[6]

The paucity of firm research results concerning whether professors tend to be intrinsically or extrinsically motivated is a serious question for further research. If faculty members are, in the main, extrinsically motivated (as much research seems to indicate), then the appraisal system and its connected rewards and punishments will provide an important tool in accomplishing organizational objectives.[7] If it is assumed that professors are intrinsically motivated, then performance appraisal and reward systems are not capable of directing performance. On the other hand, if individual faculty members differ in their motivations, and the relative strengths of their sources of motivation differ between tenure rewards and rank rewards, then the appraisal system and its reward system may be effective in directing behavior in some cases, but not in others.

The analyses offered in this book become more important as predictors of behaviors, the more professors are extrinsically motivated. All performance appraisal systems are also incentive systems if they are properly connected to rewards and punishments, that is, salaries, promotions and tenure. Intrinsic motivation, however, requires more than simply the external reward system. Internal values must be analyzed, known and/or shaped if professional activities are to be channelled into useful areas when professors are intrinsically motivated. In the case of intrinsic motivation, the ethics of the professor or university may do more to elicit behaviors than an external reward or punishment system. Further, the only collective basis upon which to gauge internal value systems is through the ethics displayed within a given organization. Internal values can be observed through self-reporting or through observation of people's activities. However, individual value systems are not something that can form the basis of policy to affect collective behavior, except to the extent that those values become adopted by the group. Ethics are group values. For any appraisal system to have utility it must account for both extrinsic and intrinsic motivation. The appraisal system is the cornerstone of channelling extrinsic motivation, and ethics are the collective internal values which channel intrinsic motivation. Consequently, an appraisal system lacking either external or internal effect is lacking in utility. Ethical performance appraisal, therefore, implies a more complete appraisal than that associated with systems that focus solely on external rewards. The completeness dimension in ethical appraisal systems is concerned with the scope of appraisal. In Chapter 3, the ethical dimensions concerned with the conduct of appraisal will be introduced.

The ethical dimensions of scope of appraisal are primarily concerned with the structure of the process and with the criteria to be used to assess performance. For example, if a professor is expected to be an effective teacher, but the appraisal system does not specify the gathering and weighing of evidence concerning instructional effectiveness and places all the weight on other factors, the scope of the evaluation has an ethical failure. The ethical failure is that the factors concerned in the appraisal are not those that were said to be expected. On the other hand, if teaching is measured using only one aspect, for example, student evaluations, and no effort is made to gather and analyze information on the other characteristics of effective teaching, the assessment is incomplete, and hence, again, unethical.

Academic leadership can do much to shape the ethics of a school or department. In turn, the ethics can modify intrinsically motivated behaviors. There are two important implications that may be drawn from the idea of leadership: leadership should probably be an important criterion for certain professorial ranks because of its importance in motivating behavior within the academic unit that cannot be reached through external systems, and leadership is an important adjunct to the appraisal system with respect to behavioral modification within the organization. Full professors and academic administrators should step forward and possess positive characteristics expected of leaders, but the question resurfaces—are people motivated to leadership intrinsically or extrinsically?

One dimension of ethical appraisal is more complete appraisal. This dimension extends to including the internal value system, including morals, ethics, leadership and other such personal values that are exhibited by professionals—particularly college professors. Unfortunately, too often, these characteristics are noticed and appraised only in their absence. Unethical conduct may be exceedingly noticeable, where consistent good citizenship is taken for granted. In this arena of performance, all of the difficulties associated with intangible outputs are in evidence. The identification of performance and its measurement, when value system based, is an exceedingly difficult proposition in performance appraisal, but also it is exceedingly important. For example, several institutions are blessed with the average teacher, average researcher, who teaches the extra section so that another faculty member can serve as president of a professional organization, will retool to teach a section of a course that is needed once every two years for the major, and does all the research for the planning committee. Too often, the average professor's contributions go unnoticed because they are not a teaching award or a book; but without these contributions the system may not be able to support other scholars gaining the recognition of a teaching award or publishing a book.

SUMMARY AND CONCLUSIONS

Performance appraisal is an important supporting activity for the accomplishment of organizational goals and to channel individual behaviors. The structure of the performance appraisal system flows directly from the goals established at each level of the academic organization. The criteria of the appraisal system must be logically connected to the goals that the organization has decided are important to its mission.

The criteria in any performance appraisal system have two dimensions. Criteria directly impact the well-being of employees through being connected to, or the basis for, the reward and punishment systems used by universities, such as salary, tenure, and promotion. The criteria contained in the appraisal system are signals to professors as to what is expected from them and how those expectations are to be translated into professional outputs. The criteria also serve a more global function in that they permit the organization to gauge how well it is accomplishing its mission at each level.

The criteria specified within a performance appraisal system serve the important function of providing incentives to professors to perform. If extrinsically motivated, professors will respond to the rewards and punishments associated with the performance appraisal systems. If intrinsically motivated, ethical considerations are the behavioral stimuli that will shape professional behaviors. To have a more complete system of appraisal, both internal values and external stimuli must be targeted for assessment.

NOTES

1. See F. J. Landy and J. L. Farr, *The Measurement of Work Performance: Methods, Theory and Applications* (New York: Academic Press, 1983), for further discussion.

2. R. W. Beatty, "Competitive Human Resource Advantage Through Strategic Management of Performance," *Human Resource Planning* (Summer 1989), pp. 179–94.

3. A. Mohrman, S. M. Resnick-West and E. E. Lawler, *Designing Performance Appraisal Systems* (San Francisco: Jossey-Bass, 1990), pp. 2–10.

4. M. Sweeney, M. J. Barr, J. J. Siegfried, J. E. Raymond and J. T. Wilkinson, "The Structure of the Introductory Course in the United States," *Journal of Economic Education* (Fall 1983), pp. 68–75.

5. For example, see W. E. Becker, "Professorial Behavior Given a Stochastic Reward Structure," *American Economic Review* (December 1979), pp. 1010–17.

6. For example, see L. Rose, "Adjustment of Student Ratings of Teachers for Extrinsic Influences," *Journal of Economic Education* (Spring 1975), pp. 129–32.

7. See Becker, "Professional Behavior Given a Stochastic Reward Structure."

Chapter 3

Ethics and Evidence in Academic Performance Appraisal

Academic ethics, as is true of almost all callings and professions today, have come under closer scrutiny in recent years.[1] There are several reasons why ethics have taken a place of prominence in social discourse. Scandals have rocked the government, businesses and even professional sports in this country. Scandal is not something new; since the beginnings of recorded history there has been scandal. The increasing frequency with which scandal seems to rock the government, businesses and professional sports has shaken confidence in many of the nation's institutions. The decline in confidence, together with increased institutional complexity, has raised speculation that the nation is in the midst of an ethical crisis from which academe is not immune.[2]

The breakdown of confidence in the ethical conduct of institutions is also demonstrated by increased litigation. The suspicion that accompanies the breakdown of ethics, whether real or perceived, creates a climate in which lawsuits arise. The general increase in litigation concerning employment issues, especially discrimination and performance appraisal, is especially troublesome. However, the adoption and enforcement of sound ethical standards are an alternative to increasing rates of litigation. If ethical standards are adopted and applied, then confidence in institutions rises and less actionable conduct occurs. In short, ethical conduct not only keeps people from approaching the boundaries of liability, but also demonstrates trustworthiness, which eases suspicion.

The purpose of this chapter is to provide a basis for the understanding of why ethics are critical to appropriate performance appraisal in academe and of the multifaceted role ethics play in institutions of higher education. Ethics play a significant role at both the macro and micro levels of performance appraisal. At the micro level, ethical conduct is typically expected of a professor, however ethics may be defined within the institution. If the professor engages in unethical conduct, such conduct is generally taken into account in any evaluation of the professor's performance. On the macro level, the construction of an appraisal system must be founded on ethical considerations. The ethical foundations of an appraisal system must include several characteristics. These characteristics are: fair warning of what is expected, appropriate standards on which appraisal must occur, a fair and rational procedure within which appraisal occurs, and due process for appeal of adverse evaluations. These four cornerstones of ethical appraisal systems are a different dimension of the ethics described in the preceding chapter. Completeness of the appraisal, as discussed in Chapter 1, is concerned with the scope of appraisal. The four cornerstones are concerned with the conduct of the appraisal. Each of these components of ethical faculty appraisal will be examined in turn in the following sections of this chapter.

FAIR WARNING

The missions of universities, their component colleges and other sub-units vary widely. Academe is a dynamic institution and the expectations and missions of colleges and universities have always been subject to change. The recent financial crises that have overtaken many state-supported and private universities have increased the intensity with which the roles and missions of academic organizations have changed. What a faculty member is expected to do is generally a function of the mission of the school in which he or she holds an academic appointment. Therefore, changes in mission will also frequently change what is expected of the academic appointee.

A great deal has been written concerning the ethics of employer-employee relations. Specifically, contracts, implicit or explicit, must be ethical if an array of personnel problems and legal difficulties are to be avoided. Drake and Drake, for example, delineate the four requirements for an employment contract to be ethical:

1. Both of the parties to a contract must have full knowledge of the nature of the agreement they are entering.

2. Neither party to a contract may intentionally misrepresent the facts of the contractual situation to the other party.

3. Neither party to the contract must be forced to enter the contract under duress or coercion.

4. The contract must not bind the parties to an immoral act.[3]

Drake and Drake examine generic employment contacts, but the principles apply to academe. Even if a written contract is not signed, there will be expectations conveyed to prospective faculty members. These expectations must be as complete as possible and, where feasible, should be reduced to writing. They might be conveyed in a faculty handbook or a set of regulations that are given to all prospective faculty members.

Intentions concerning the directions of the university, school, or department should also be made clear. Many schools go through transition periods. For example, it is not uncommon for business schools to set as a goal accreditation under the standards of the American Assembly of Collegiate Schools of Business (AACSB). For many schools that have a primary focus on teaching, the research, personnel and curricular requirements of AACSB accreditation cause a substantial departure from historic goals and manners of operation. Very frequently, research will become much more important to these schools than it had been in the past. The political difficulties associated with such a change will often be substantial. Those faculty members whose efforts had been concentrated primarily in the classroom will often feel threatened by the increased importance of research. As a result, prospective new faculty members may receive mixed signals about the importance of research in promotion and tenure decisions. In fact, the dean and department chairs may even misrepresent the relative importance of research to a candidate so as to attract someone with a publication record or potential to do scholarly research. The misrepresentation may not be intentional, but may reflect the administrators' own political difficulties. In several cases observed by the authors, deans have assured candidates that research is of primary importance and that personnel decisions will be weighted heavily toward research in assessing a faculty member's performance. When the candidates are hired, they find later that salary increments and promotion and tenure decisions use research productivity only as a marginal variable because the faculty, in aggregate, has not accepted the fact that research is of substantial importance in accreditation decisions. The end result is the creation of an academic culture which is lacking an important ethical dimension, consistency.

It is rare in academe that an individual faculty member will be subjected to duress or coercion in the negotiation of a contract. It does happen, however. A common example is one in which a man and wife (both Ph.D.s) are both employed at the same institution. Occasionally, salary increment decisions are affected by the fact that both are employees. Some perverse notion of equity may be used to justify giving one or the other a lower than earned increment because the university has both on the payroll. This type of reasoning is illustrative of a subtle form of duress. The fact that spouses are members of the same university's faculty is irrelevant and the implicit restraint of joint mobility is being used to disadvantage one or both. Such behavior constitutes unethical performance appraisal because, again, there is an inconsistency in the way in which individuals are treated.

Immoral contractual requirements are rare. In university athletic programs, however, examples of binding individuals to immoral conduct can be found. Southern Methodist University, the University of Nevada-Las Vegas and the University of Oklahoma have all made headlines in the sports pages because of activities that violate NCAA rules. One should question whether the goal of university athletics is to have winning football and basketball traditions regardless of cost. Pressures from financial contributors, alumni and others to win place coaching staffs in the position of win or perish at too many institutions. If winning requires the acquisition of talent, and competition for that talent is too keen, then advantages in the recruiting process can be had by going outside of the rules. To "cheat" in recruiting is an unethical act and certainly can contribute to the "We're number one" mentality. Couple this win-at-all-costs mentality with the financial pressures of running an intercollegiate football or basketball program and it is little wonder that there have been serious moral deficiencies in college athletics.

It is also interesting to note that Drake and Drake state, "[t]hese ethical requirements apply to initial contracts as well as to any changes made in the contracts; that is, to the corporate culture at the time an employee is hired as well as management actions taken to change the existing culture." Schools moving from one set of objectives to another have certain obligations. These obligations include "fair warning" and sufficient time to adjust before promotion and tenure decisions are made. To establish a new set of criteria, which differ substantially from previous criteria, the year that a promotion or tenure decision is made lacks basic fairness and is, therefore, unethical. It is unethical because a faculty member may now be evaluated using standards he or she had no way of knowing would be applied.

WHAT ARE APPROPRIATE STANDARDS?

Standards are the guideposts to decision making. The use of standards is necessary to make the evaluation process consistent and valid. Since 1972, educational institutions face all the same legal obligations imposed on private business by Title VII of the 1964 Civil Rights Act.[4] Consistent standards are required to assure legal compliance[5] and an ethical evaluation process.[6]

Standards are of two varieties, objective and subjective. In objective systems, there is the obligation to gather data, and then to compare the evidence with some explicit set of performance criteria to determine the acceptability of the performance. In subjective systems, an administrator or committee is charged with the responsibility to determine whether a faculty member has achieved a level of performance consistent with the granting of tenure, promotion, or an appropriate salary level.

In the case of subjective standards, the determinations to be made will be on the basis of evidence, much the same as objective standards, but the decisions will be the professional opinions of those doing the assessment. The use of professional opinion as the basis for weighing evidence requires there to be some specific professional characteristics identified that the decision maker(s) must possess to occupy the decision-making position. Without the possession of the required characteristics of the decision makers to make professional opinions, there is a substantial limit to what can be assessed. The problem then arises with the scope of the assessment. If evaluators do not possess the professional competence to assess performance, they must seek outside guidance or risk ethical dilemma concerning the scope of assessment.

Objective standards run the same risk as subjective standards in that the processes used to quantify standards or to make them objective may not capture aspects of the performance that are important to the performance appraisal. For example, if someone is required to publish five refereed journal articles to be tenured, there is no mention of quality of the journal, professional contributions represented by the research, number of authors or several other aspects that may be of substantial importance in assessing research performance.

Controversy abounds concerning whether objective or subjective standards are better. Objective standards offer the benefit that once the evidence is gathered, it is simply compared with specified levels of performance in making a personnel decision. Critics of objective systems are quick to point out that the performance levels identified in objective systems are very frequently established subjectively, thereby reducing the objective system to nothing more than a quantified subjective system.

Subjective systems offer the benefit of leaving the system in the hands of professionals who can assess the total package of professional conduct without being limited to quantifiable or objective measures of an individual faculty member's performance. Critics of subjective systems question the humaneness and the professional nature of these systems. They contend that subjective methods of evaluation offer the potential for games of political intrigue and skullduggery.

A few schools have even opted for more elaborate systems where objective standards are used, but the guideposts are left to be determined empirically. For example, rather than leave to collective action the requirements for a personnel action, a faculty will determine what schools are comparable and use the averages for previous personnel decisions to set guideposts. This is done to remove elements of subjectivity one step further from the establishment of objective standards.

There is potential for both good and evil no matter which approach to evaluation is chosen. No matter which form of standards is employed there are a few basic principles that must be in evidence. These are: any standard used must be a valid consideration that is specifically related to the professional requirements of the job; faculty members must be made aware of what they must accomplish in order to gain promotions, tenure or salary increases; if either objective or subjective standards are used, they must be based on reliable and valid evidence; if objective standards are used, they must be constructed in such a manner as to account for the critical aspects of performance and cannot be a single measure (unless a single performance is required); and if subjective standards are used, the persons making the subjective assessment must have the credible expertise and the professional position to make such assessments valid.

The five principles of performance assessment follow directly from the four ethical cornerstones of evaluation. These five principles of assessment are the characteristics of an assessment system necessary to operationalize the four ethical cornerstones.

EVIDENTIAL PROCEDURES: FAIR AND REASONABLE

The evaluation procedures used to gather and weigh evidence about professional activity and to assess the merit of that activity must be fair and reasonable. Fairness and reasonableness are difficult characteristics to precisely define. At the extremes, their absence is clearly noticed (normally) and their consistent presence is generally noticed. The gray area in between the extremes is where fairness and/or reasonableness become difficult to identify. The one generalization that is always true is that fairness and reasonableness exist in the eye of the beholder. There are issues that directly influence the perceptions of reasonableness and fairness concerning the evidence used in appraisal. These issues involve the discovery of evidence, challenges to adverse elements of the record and the role of evidence in performance assessment. Each of these issues will be reviewed in the following paragraphs in this section.

Discovery of Evidence

Objective performance appraisal systems are driven by data and quantitative standards. In the final analysis, the success of an objective system depends crucially upon the quality of the data collected and the appropriateness of the standards employed. Discovery of evidence can rarely be accomplished in a static sense, but is a dynamic process. That is, data cannot generally be acquired at some point in time, but must be gathered consistently during an evaluation period.

The data-gathering process must be clearly identified, and the information must be accessible to those expected to collect it. For example, when an individual is initially employed, the types of data they should gather and maintain to support personnel decisions should be clearly identified. If course syllabi, examinations and lesson plans are necessary to support a case for competence in teaching, these items must be identified so as to permit adequate opportunity to maintain these items over a period of years. If student, peer or expert in-class evaluations are required, there must be fair warning so that these evaluations can be made and the evidence provided.

Frequently, institutions will not identify the specific data to be gathered but will identify elements of instruction that must be examined and leave the identification and gathering of data to the individual. Where such systems are used, it is necessary to identify the types of information that decision makers regard as inappropriate and the types that decision makers have given credibility. Annual reviews of untenured professors or other professors eligible to apply for promotion can serve to identify the strengths and weaknesses of the data gathered each year.

The data gathered must be from credible sources. There is considerable controversy over the reliability and validity of student questionnaires.[7] Peer evaluation of instruction is also limited by the credible expertise in teaching possessed by the peer called upon to evaluate. If these types of data are relied upon, they should be controlled for bias and their validity and reliability must be demonstrable.

The record of evidence gathered by the candidate or an appropriate administrator must also be safeguarded from tampering or loss. Annual reviews and documentation of claimed expertise or quality provide a running record of evidence on which promotion and tenure cases can be based. Maintenance of these records is essential for the orderly processing of these cases.

Challenges to Adverse Elements of the Record

Criteria for performance assessment vary, and they may be subjective or objective. Even under objective standards, the types of evidence that may be gathered may differ significantly from one department to another and from one faculty member to another. This is because not every faculty member can be expected to have the same strengths and weaknesses. Thus, not every faculty member should be required to produce exactly the same evidence of instructional effectiveness, research productivity or quality of professional service. It is true that a certain degree of consistency should be required to assure efficient assessments and that there should be some inherent consistency because of the similarity of teaching and research activities. However, forcing everyone into exactly the same mold ignores academic freedom and individual diversity. Without the opportunity to challenge the admission and weighing of evidence, there is no assurance that a faculty member's performance assessment will be perceived as reasonable and fair.

Opportunities for challenges to what may be perceived to be adverse evidence must be provided in an appraisal system to assure that a faculty member has a chance to present his or her case fully. Without the opportunity to challenge evidence, the evaluation process may become tainted because of evidence that was not appropriate to the assessment. If a faculty member is permitted to challenge the use of certain elements of the evidential record, he or she will have the opportunity to argue how the evidence should be viewed by decision makers. Whether the faculty member's position prevails or not, at least the decision makers have an opportunity to hear the person's opinion concerning that evidence, and the process creates, if not the substance, at least the appearance of being reasonable and fair.

Besides ethical concerns for perceived fairness and reasonableness, there is another reason to allow opportunities to challenge evidence. Under either an objective or subjective process, decisions will be no better than the evidence upon which they are based. The "quality" of personnel decisions is therefore dependent upon having the best possible record of evidence. To permit challenges to evidence assures that the record will be subject to closer scrutiny. Open procedures that are subject to outside scrutiny eliminate much of the evil associated with doing important things behind "closed doors"—hence the sunshine laws adopted by the majority of the states. Nothing can guarantee that the evidence upon which decisions must be based will be optimal, but safeguards should be provided when possible.

Role of Evidence

Both subjective and objective evaluation schemes must identify the role that evidence is to play in making personnel decisions. In a subjective scheme, the decision maker may be required to *consider evidence*, or must make a decision *based on the preponderance of credible evidence*. In an objective system, there may be no consideration by a decision maker except to ascertain if the evidence is of the quantity and quality demanded by the personnel policy. In other cases, however, the decision maker may be given some latitude to determine whether there is sufficient evidence to meet a specific requirement.

For example, in the appraisal of research there may be an assignment of points for articles in particular journals. The role of the decision maker may be minimal here if the acquisition of research points is the only determining factor. On the other hand, the quality of journals may be identified and the requirement may be stated that a candidate have published the results of original research in refereed, quality journals sufficient to establish a national reputation as a scholar. The evidence may be objective, but the standard is certainly subjective, unless there is a clear definition of a national reputation. What evidence is to be considered and what role it is to play must be clearly identified. Otherwise, the evaluation process is not predictable, and hence does not provide the candidate with sufficient information to know what is required. Without knowledge of what is required, the system reduces to one with the potential for arbitrary and capricious determinations, which are unethical by nature.

DUE PROCESS

Due process, in a legal sense, is nothing more than being given reasonable access to the processes and procedures specified by statute or, in this case, policy. Due process generally implies a certain element of basic fairness, but fairness and due process are not the same concepts. Generally, in employment matters, if the personnel policies do not provide for due process, then an employee must seek redress in the court under some theory of contract or discriminatory treatment. Most universities have seen fit to provide for due process in personnel policies in general and specifically in matters concerning performance assessment.

Appeals of adverse decisions almost always become embroiled in disagreements as to the fairness of the decision and the process used to arrive at the result. Due process requires that an individual be entitled to whatever review or appeal process will guarantee compliance with the institution's policies and procedures. There is no standard method by which a university has provided for due process. Universities have opted for an array of different approaches to the issue of due process. Nonunion universities typically rely on processes that are very informal and not final and binding such as peer review, committee review or administrative review. Some universities permit a committee or peer review process followed by a second step at the highest administrative level. It is almost unheard of for a nonunion university to have adopted what is commonly understood as a grievance procedure. In unionized universities, it is common to observe standard grievance procedures where there is a multiple-step grievance procedure. Some even permit committee partici- pation rather than solely administrative determination before proceeding to final and binding arbitration. The difference between union and non- union approaches is not a matter of due process but simply a matter of effectiveness in maintaining the perception of fairness and high morale. As the presidential commission appointed by Truman in 1947 found, the multiple-step, formalized process that culminates in final and binding arbitration is almost always perceived as being more fair than internal processes and is associated with better employee morale.

Peer review is generally accomplished by an elected committee of faculty members, which operates without formal rules of evidence or procedures, and whose purpose it is to review actions affecting individual faculty members. There is no requirement that the individuals serving in peer review be neutrals, and there is no assumed expertise.

In arbitration, a neutral third party who is assumed to have a degree of expertise in the subject matter takes on the role of decision maker. Arbitration utilizes rules of evidence that are informal, but generally more formal than those found in peer review.

Committee review is generally undertaken by a specific committee that stands for the purpose of assuring due process. The committee may not substitute its judgment for that of those who have already decided. Unlike peer review, committee review is restricted to examination of the process by which a decision is reached, and not to the merits of the case specifically.

Administrative review is normally built into the evaluation process, but may specify that an individual may appeal an adverse decision to a specific individual administrator who then has the responsibility to investigate and determine whether due process was violated. Some universities, such as Michigan State University and the University of Iowa, have established ombudsman processes where an individual faculty member hears the complaints of others and is charged with the responsibility of assuring the fairness of evaluation processes. The ombudsman is generally in a position to attempt to mediate differences, but mediation failing, is sometimes granted the authorities of an arbitrator. (The ombudsman at the University of Iowa is Anthony Sinicropi, a respected Labor Arbitrator.) Most ombudsman systems in major universities utilize the services of a professional labor arbitrator.

Without due process requirements, the evaluation process can take place outside public view. The evaluation process must be capable of withstanding close scrutiny. Due process guarantees that such scrutiny is available to right procedural wrongs which can taint personnel decisions. Unless due process guarantees are assured in the evaluation policy, there is no method of insuring compliance with policy. Thus, unethical deviations from an otherwise appropriate evaluation system may occur.

CHANGE AND REVIEW OF POLICIES

Written evaluation policies and periodic review of those policies to assure congruence with institutional goals and objectives are a necessary part of introducing reason to the policy. Unfortunately, strategic management is something with which many institutions have difficulty. Without an effective strategic plan, the goals and objectives of individual administrators or cliques within the faculty may be substituted for institutional goals. Arbitrary and capricious behavior occasionally results, making the planning process more political than scholarly. To the extent that the standards of evaluation must reflect institutional goals, strategic planning is a prerequisite activity to establishing evaluation policies and criteria consistent with those goals.

As previously stated, the appraisal system must be tailored to the school's mission. Personnel decisions must be consistent with the requirements of the school's appraisal system. Consequently, personnel decisions are usually made in a manner to further the mission of the school. As change impacts the missions of the school, there must be review and revision of the personnel policies, including each aspect of the assessment system so that the mission is appropriately supported. On the other hand, faculty members' salary increments, promotion and tenure depend critically upon the standards employed. There is a delicate balance to be struck in protecting the rights of faculty members and permitting the school to progress. It is the ethical environment in which this balance is sought that will determine whether the interests of the school and the interests of faculty members will be consistent.

SUMMARY AND CONCLUSIONS

At the same time that it protects faculty rights, ethical performance appraisal is an important supporting mechanism for the accomplishment of the institution's mission. Without an academic environment that identifies and assures faculty rights, high turnover rates, lack of commitment and fear can permeate the faculty, thereby reducing its effectiveness. There are two dimensions of ethics in academe: micro and macro. The micro dimensions apply to individual professorial or administrative conduct, and the macro dimensions apply to policies of a unit and its conduct. Both dimensions must be considered to have effective and ethical performance appraisal. The policies must have ethical safeguards, and the persons charged with the responsibility of administering the policies must behave ethically.

Ethical performance appraisal is generic. The four basic characteristics of ethical employment contracts apply across all occupations. These characteristics are: (1) that the contract be complete and known, (2) that there be no misrepresentations, (3) there can be no duress or coercion to enter into the relation and (4) there can be no requirement to commit immoral acts.

NOTES

1. Numerous articles have been published concerning professorial and institutional ethics in academe in the last seven years. For a small selection, see: Bruce Wilshire, "Can the University Defend the Values upon Which it Stands?," *Journal of Higher Education*, vol. 58, no. 3 (May/June 1987), pp. 249–60; and Daniel Callahan, "Should There Be an Academic Code of Ethics?," *Journal of Higher Education*, vol. 53, no. 3 (May/June 1982), pp. 336–44 (one of a symposium on the subject of ethics appearing in that volume and number of the *Journal of Higher Education*).

2. George Schurr, "Toward a Code of Ethics for Academics," *Journal of Higher Education*, vol. 53, no. 3 (May/June 1982), pp. 318–34.

3. Bruce H. Drake and Eileen Drake, "Ethical and Legal Aspects of Managing Corporate Cultures," *California Management Review*, vol. 30, no. 1, pp. 107–23.

4. Ben Taylor and Fred Witney, *Labor Relations Law*, 4th ed. (Englewood Cliffs, N.J.: Prentice-Hall, 1983), p. 664.

5. The EEOC and the courts have established that a valid and consistent application of bona fide employment requirements is the only acceptable basis for hiring, retention and promotion decisions; for example, see *Dothard v. Rawlinson*, 433 U.S. 321 (1977), *County of Washington v. Alberta Gunther*, 101 S.Ct. 751 (1981), and *Cleveland Board of Education v. La Fleur*, 414 U.S. 631 (1974).

6. Vernon R. Loucks, Jr., "A CEO Looks at Ethics," *Business Horizons* (March/April 1987), pp. 2–6.

7. See Chapter 5 for further discussion.

Part II

Performance Appraisal Criteria

Chapter 4

Assessing What Professors Do: Citizenship, Research, Service and Teaching

What do professors do? It is not an easy question to answer. One generality that is true is that faculty members in colleges and universities are different from teachers in high schools in that more is expected than simply teaching and maintaining order. Most colleges and universities expect that faculty members will engage in professional service and research, along with teaching and meeting basic citizenship requirements. Before turning our attention to the specifics of teaching, research, service and citizenship, a brief examination of the mix of professorial activities is presented in the first section of this chapter.

As discussed in previous chapters, there are differences in missions across academic institutions. The variations in mission result in variations in what is expected of the faculty as a whole. Within specific academic units, there may also be differences in what is expected of faculty members. The variation in expectations across institutions and across faculty members within institutions complicates the analysis of what professors do. The planning function of academic institutions is, therefore, of critical importance to ethical and proper evaluation of faculty members' productivity. The planning function will be given a brief analysis in the second section of this chapter.

Teaching, research and service have been the subjects of considerable research and can be meaningfully addressed from the given body of knowledge. Unfortunately, almost nothing known to these authors has been written about citizenship within the academic department. Rather than to ignore the subject of citizenship, some brief remarks concerning the strategic importance and role of citizenship are included in the chapter on service evaluation.

MIX OF PROFESSIONAL ACTIVITIES

There are several debates in academe concerning the role and inter-relations of teaching, research and service. One debate has centered on the relation between teaching and research. Three propositions have been advanced: (1) that teaching and research are independent activities and have no necessary relation, (2) that teaching and research are complementary (i.e., good researchers make good teachers) and (3) that teaching and research are substitutes (i.e., teaching and research are not necessarily compatible activities, and too often time is taken away from teaching to become more effective in research).[1]

The debate has been joined on several levels. There are those who present empirical evidence (discussed in the research chapter) to support their contentions and some bring theoretical constructs to the arena as support (again, discussed in the research chapter). What all of this controversy conclusively demonstrates is that there is disagreement on the effects of mixing teaching, research and service, and that there is evidence that supports each of the major contentions to be found in the literature.

The debate does not present such a terrible dilemma. Whether teaching and research are compatible functions is an institution-specific, and perhaps even an individual-specific, question. The answer depends on what goals and missions the institution establishes for itself, as well as the talents and abilities of specific individuals. In short, the authors contend that there are valid points on each side of this debate. The observed evidence and the conclusions drawn are probably accurate in each case, but there is an underlying phenomenon that has heretofore been missed. First, the observations are probably due to the planning, performance appraisal, and reward/punishment policies of the institution. Second, there are undoubtedly individual faculty members whose talents and abilities are far more consistent with excellence in either teaching or research, but who cannot do both well. It is also probably true that there is a cadre of faculty members who are both good teachers and researchers.

What is clear is there is no single mix of professional activities that is appropriate to all academic institutions. As previously stated, the missions established for the institution will provide substantial guidance in establishing goals and objectives to be attained, hence the mix of professional activities within the university and its subunits. The mission statement also serves as a guide to the establishment of appropriate performance appraisal. Because the performance appraisal system serves notice of what is expected from faculty members, the limits for the mix of professional activities will also be set by the performance appraisal system. In turn, the appraisal system is a major component in informing faculty of what is expected and motivating them to an organized effort toward achieving the institution's goals and objectives.

The systematic examination of evidence concerning the quality and quantity of professional accomplishments is the basis for performance appraisal. The mix of those professional activities will, in large measure, also specify the bounds of the performance appraisal system. If only one professional activity is expected or is predictive of the quantity and quality of all other professional activities, it will be necessary to gather and analyze evidence concerning only that activity. If a range of activities is expected then several types of evidence will be required. Consequently, the range of evaluation must be examined to determine what must be measured.

Because there is generally more than one activity expected of professors, there must be an identification of the proportions of activities expected. With purely objective standards, weights are often applied to quantify the mix of activities expected. For example, if a quantified standard is used where 5 is the best rating and 0 is the worst, then weights are necessary to determine the total evaluation. In such a system, if a weight of .1 is assigned to service and citizenship, .3 to research, and .6 to teaching, then ten percent of total evaluation will be accounted for by service and citizenship, sixty percent by teaching and the remainder for research. Whether subjective or objective standards are used, if there is a mix of activities there must also be a weighting scheme to translate the component portions of the evaluation to a total performance evaluation.

For the organizational level, the weighting scheme must reflect the relative importance of the goals of that academic unit. Weights for individual faculty members may be varied to take advantage of an individual's relative strengths and weaknesses, but this flexibility in assigning weights is constrained. The operable constraint is that the summation of the weights across faculty members must total to what is expected of the academic unit. For example, if the academic unit's mission is about equally split between research and teaching, individual weights that result in little or no weight being assigned to either teaching or research results in incongruence between individual performances and the unit's total performance. In such cases the weights must be changed for individuals or the institution needs to rethink its mission.

Are Teaching, Research, Service and Citizenship Related?

Publish or perish may be the easiest of all performance based appraisal systems to administer. Each year an administrator or committee adds up the number of publications for each faculty member and awards salary increases on the basis of who published the most. After some specified period of time, generally seven years, if a faculty member published an adequate number of quality studies, tenure and promotion are awarded. In fact, there are several institutions that currently use such a system.

Publish or perish is completely appropriate if publication in the leading journals is all that needs to occur to accomplish the school's mission. If the institution or relevant subunit has no goals or mission in teaching or service, or does not expect good citizenship, then publish or perish may serve it well. Even the most ardent proponents of publish or perish in academic departments, however, recognize that most academic institutions have a teaching or service portion of their mission and require good citizenship. Further, if teaching or service is a portion of one's duties, and good citizenship is required, then there is a logical inconsistency in ignoring the other missions. If citizenship, teaching and service are expected, they must be evaluated and weighed in the appropriate personnel decisions. Without such accountability it is unlikely that these objectives will be served. Expressed expectations in citizenship, service or teaching, if left unevaluated, serve only to mislead, unless research is viewed as predictive of quality in the three other areas.

One argument that has been advanced in support of publish or perish is that quality teaching and service can only occur when a faculty member publishes in quality journals. Such a position overstates the case. In reviewing the teaching evaluation chapter, the reader will observe that there are several educational objectives and these can be categorized in the cognitive and affective domains. Ignoring the affective domain for the moment, if research is required for one to be classified as a good teacher, then only the cognitive domain is relevant. Research and teaching both require knowledge of the subject matter; however, they require mastery of different media for that knowledge to be presented. A lecture is far different from writing for a scholarly journal, but if knowledge can be presented in both activities (an assumption most would be willing to accept), then does it not necessarily follow that a single individual will always possess both talents? In academe, competent teachers may be relatively common, but researchers with the ability to consistently publish the results of original and meaningful research may be relatively rare. It may also be that truly excellent classroom teachers are relatively rare, and researchers with the ability to get something in a refereed journal once or twice a year are relatively common.

There has been research concerning the relationship of teaching and research. There are reported results that demonstrate that teaching and research come from closely related inputs, but are separate outputs. Whether research and teaching are necessarily complementary activities is not yet conclusively demonstrated, but there is no theoretical basis or empirical evidence that demonstrates that research and teaching must be positively correlated.[2] In fact, there is evidence that strongly supports the hypothesis that professors do what they are paid to do, for the most part.[3] This suggests that professors are extrinsically motivated and respond to incentives much the same as workers in general industry. In fact, there is empirical evidence that shows that faculty members at large universities are paid for research output, but not generally compensated for quality teaching.[4] In any event, the evidence shows that excellence in research implies nothing about classroom performance.[5]

The demonstration of knowledge through publication in refereed journals shows that a faculty member is keeping abreast with at least some portion of her or his academic discipline. It does not assure that the faculty member also has the breadth of knowledge necessary to be an effective teacher in specific courses.

The same types of arguments can be offered in the service arena. There are, however, areas of service, such as funded research, consulting and technical service activities, that are clearly more closely related to research. If an expert is needed to provide the service, the reputation for excellence in scholarly pursuits is frequently used as a proxy for expertise.

Citizenship, however, is a prerequisite for being a good teacher or competent scholar. A person with a history of moral turpitude or unethical conduct is not the type of person who should be trusted with a college classroom. Honesty is also a prerequisite for being a sound scholar.

It should be noted that there are several aspects of teaching, research, service and citizenship that have common roots. The command of language skills, intellectual honesty, the ability to organize thoughts and an inquiring mind are probably necessary to be successful in the academic enterprise. There is simply nothing in the literature, however, that has been discovered that suggests that research, teaching and service have any necessary relationship in general. Consequently, each of these academic activities must be evaluated if they are a portion of the institution's mission.

PLANNING AND PROFESSORIAL OUTPUT

Planning and the resultant mission statements are the basis for account-ability, and accountability will truly determine the mix of activities professors will choose. Suppose that the mission statement states that a school is a teaching institution, but suppose no attempt to evaluate teaching is actually made. Instead, suppose the school rewards only research. Then, the mission statement to the contrary, only research will be produced. The moral is that the proper place to answer the question of what professors will do is the planning phase of academic governance.

The mission of an institution of higher learning almost always contains some mix of teaching and research. It is not uncommon for colleges and universities to also say something about service to certain external con-stituencies. In land grant schools, for example, the agriculture extension service is expected to provide assistance and expertise to farmers and the agricultural industry in general. The extension service is obviously a service function. Some urban, state and private institutions may also reserve a portion of their role for the provision of certain professional services to relevant constituencies.

Liberal arts colleges and junior colleges will often seek to provide quality classroom instruction as their primary mission, and have a mix of additional minor objectives that usually include research and service. At major state and private universities, however, teaching and research are customarily the central missions.

Planning produces mission statements, which are dynamic entities. The planning documents of universities are broad and wondrous things that speak to furthering the frontiers of knowledge and the betterment of mankind. It is at the college or school level that the mission statement begins to operationalize the goals that form the basis for accountability. At the college or school level, specific statements concerning the mix of professorial duties are generally found. Many schools and colleges also permit still greater specificity of mission for smaller academic subunits such as departments. In other words, at the university level some general statements about the total university effort will be made. At the school or college level specific mixes of teaching, research and service will be identified. The departments may have some additional latitude in more clearly defining the types and amounts of teaching, research and service to be performed.

The mission statement, however, is of little significance until the evaluation, reward and punishment mechanisms are in place. To implement a mission statement requires that accountability be created and appropriately administered.

INDIVIDUAL FACULTY MEMBERS AND THEIR DIFFERENCES

Each professor brings strengths and weaknesses to academe just like any other professional. The authors are convinced that individual faculty differences may be one of the important determinants in the debate concerning whether teaching and research are substitutes, complements or simply independent. Among faculty members, some may have multiple talents while others possess only a singular talent. This difference in endowments might certainly explain why there is empirical evidence to support every known position concerning the relation between teaching and research. What has been perceived as an allocation of effort phenomenon may be simply observed endowments of abilities. The existence of significant individual differences has notable implications for planning and for performance appraisal. Planning to obtain excellent research from good teachers makes no sense, unless those good teachers are also excellent researchers. The planning function should take into account known differences among faculty members. Utilize good teachers/poor researchers in the classroom; utilize good researchers/poor teachers in research activities; and count your blessings for the good teachers/good researchers that may be present on your faculty.

SUMMARY AND CONCLUSIONS

There is evidence to suggest that there are relationships between teaching, research and service effectiveness. However, the evidence does not suggest that there is a necessary positive correlation between teaching and research. There are several complementary activities that are exhibited in all three professional activities, but there is little evidence that suggests that these inputs extend to academic outputs.

The planning process is where accountability begins. The mission statements established for and by the institution and its subunits should identify the proper issues for evaluation. Planning and the establishment of appropriate missions require accountability if the mission is to be accomplished. Accountability occurs only if there are effective and proper evaluation criteria and processes adopted.

NOTES

1. William Becker, "The University Professor as a Utility Maximizer and Producer of Learning, Research and Income," *Journal of Human Resources* (1974), pp. 107–15.

2. See V. W. Voeks, "Publications and Teaching Effectiveness," *Journal of Higher Education* (April 1962), pp. 212–18; and J. R. Hayes, "Research, Teaching and Faculty Fate," *Science* (April 16, 1971), pp. 227–30, for further discussion.

3. See William Becker, "Professorial Behavior Given a Stochastic Reward Structure," *American Economic Review* (December 1979), pp. 1010–17; and J. J. Siegfried and K. J. White, "Teaching and Publishing as Determinants of Academic Salaries," *Journal of Economic Education* (Spring 1973), pp. 90–99, for further discussion.

4. David A. Katz, "Faculty Salaries, Rates of Promotion, and Productivity at a Large University," *American Economic Review* (June 1973), pp. 469–77.

5. See J. A. Yunker and J. W. Marlin, "Performance Evaluation of College and University Faculty: An Economic Perspective," *Educational Administration Quarterly*, vol. 20 (1984), pp. 9–37.

Chapter 5

The Evaluation of Teaching in Universities

The gathering of data for the appraisal of teaching requires the active cooperation of individual faculty members. Commitment to quality teaching and the assessment of instructional effectiveness are therefore necessary prerequisites to an effective program of instructional assessment. Intrinsically motivated teachers will often take leadership roles in gaining the requisite commitments; however, extrinsically motivated teachers may have to see the clear connection between the reward and punishment system and participation in assessment activities before they enthusiastically cooperate.

At almost every institution of higher education, teaching is considered one of the primary missions. Consequently, it is a major element in faculty appraisal.[1] Yet the evaluation of teaching is a controversial topic. There are those that believe that teaching can be effectively defined and measured.[2] Some argue that the definition and measurement of effective teaching are far more ambiguous than the majority would have you believe and are not subject to simple valuative schemes.[3] What is certainly true of most universities is that, too often, the evaluation of teaching is relatively unsystematic.[4] Because of the multi-attribute nature of instructional effectiveness, its assessment must be undertaken in a systematic manner.

The evaluation of teaching has also been the subject of study since the 1920s. Several hundreds of papers had been published on the topic before the mid-1970s.[5] Even with this substantial body of literature, there appears to be little agreement on how to define and measure effective teaching in colleges and universities. The evaluation of teaching has certainly been a controversial subject outside of the fields of education, particularly when a single measure such as student questionnaires has been the sole attempt to appraise teaching performance. As Marlin and Niss have noted:

> Teachers who have received high student evaluations in the past will find them to be valid measures of good teaching. Teachers who have received low student evaluations in the past will find them to be laughably insignificant.[6]

Perhaps this principle (the Marlin/Niss Principle) articulates the unavoidable political reality associated with student evaluations of instruction. Nevertheless, other methods are available that permit evidence of effective teaching to be obtained. Because teaching is a multidimensional activity, these methods require that multiple dimensions of the activity be examined. That means that several sources of information will be required, each focused on a specific aspect of instructional performance or to corroborate other sources of evidence with reliability or validity limitations.

The purpose of this chapter is to examine the evaluation of teaching in universities and colleges. The multiple dimensions of teaching will be examined in the first section of this chapter before turning our attention to the evaluation of instruction. The sections on evaluation of teaching include an examination of the following methods: self-evaluation by professor, student evaluation of instruction, colleague and administrator evaluations and external assessment of teaching.

TEACHING: WHAT IS IT?

In a general sense, teaching is imparting knowledge and skills to others. This definition, however, lacks specificity. Without specificity, it is almost impossible to set standards and develop processes that permit the appraisal of the activity. Accordingly, a more specific definition of teaching is necessary. Borrowing from (and adding to) Saunders and Walstad, the following definition is offered:

> *Teaching is the activity that organizes and facilitates the activities that cause learning.* Learning is the acquisition and retention of knowledge and habits of thought in a way that permits them to be employed in a useful way after the initial exposure has been terminated.[7] (italics not in original)

Teaching therefore requires the effective transmittal of knowledge and habits so that the students may acquire and retain them. Without the retention of knowledge and habits the students cannot rely upon education to serve their future needs.

LEARNING THEORIES

The examination of teaching as an activity has been organized along learning theory lines. There are several theories of learning. Each of these theories focuses on different aspects of the acquisition and processing of information presented to people. The major schools of learning theory are the behaviorists, the gestalt theorists and the information-processing theorists.

These schools of thought disagree about how learning occurs. The behaviorists focus on rewards and punishments for certain outcomes.[8] Teaching in this view is simply a matter of reinforcement for proper reactions to various stimuli.

The gestalt theorists (also called the cognitive-structuralist school) focus on the rearrangement of previously learned concepts and experiences to deal with new experiences and concepts.[9] In other words, previous knowledge, even of simple concepts, can be combined and extended to deal with new situations and concepts.

Neither the behaviorists nor the gestalt theorists are concerned about what happens in a person's mind when learning occurs. The mind is treated as a black box. These models simply concentrate on the inputs and their associated outputs.

The information-processing school does focus on what occurs in the human mind.[10] The information-processing activities in the mind are thought to convert information received into short-term memory. Short-term memory can then either allow the information to die or transform the information into long-term memory. Learning occurs when information is stored in long-term memory.

The approach to learning and consequent teaching activities associated with each of these schools of learning theory differ significantly. For example, behaviorists may focus on the incentive system created for students to learn and how well the incentive system was administered by the teacher. On the other hand, gestalt theorists may wish to focus more of their efforts on guiding students to the discovery of certain logical constructs and their use. Both the gestalt theorists and behaviorists may be accused by the information theorists of failing to provide the control necessary to bring information to long-term memory.

Without an accepted general theory of learning, teaching becomes a somewhat ambiguous activity. The lack of a general theory, however, does not mean that it cannot be defined and evaluated in some meaningful fashion. If learning theory fails to provide a specific answer that is universally accepted, then at least the evaluation of instruction can be made ethical, consistent with what is known. In this context, it is important that teachers be informed of what outcomes are deemed to be evidence of effective teaching. If the faculty has specific information concerning what is expected, then evaluation can still be ethical, even in the absence of a universally accepted definition of effective teaching.

What is defined as effective teaching must still have some sound basis. Opinions abound concerning what constitutes effective teaching; however, the specific standards by which effective teaching is defined and evaluated should come from the body of knowledge that has been acquired.

DOMAINS OF LEARNING

There are two domains in which teaching is important. Educators typically classify learning outcomes into the cognitive domain and the affective domain. Objectives, hence standards for evaluation, are properly identified within this framework.

The cognitive domain deals with issues such as knowledge, skills and mastery of concepts. The cognitive domain contains objectives that are specifically related to the subject matter of the course. For example, being able to define terms, reason through problems and interpret information are cognitive objectives. There are six basic categories of cognitive objectives.[11] From the lowest to the highest level, the cognitive objectives are:

1. knowledge,
2. comprehension,
3. applications,
4. analysis,
5. synthesis and
6. evaluation.

The lowest level of cognitive objective is knowledge. The recognition, recall and identification of material are what constitute knowledge. The next highest level is comprehension which requires the student to interpret, summarize, translate or explain the meaning of the knowledge acquired. Applications represents the ability to use the material the student has comprehended to produce or predict something. Analysis requires that the material comprehended be broken down into component parts, separated from other materials, and its organizational structure observed. Synthesis requires the ability to put the analyzed parts together to form a new idea or product. Evaluation is the ability to judge the internal and external value of the knowledge. The affective domain of teaching is concerned with student reactions to the subject. Such things are motivation, feelings and emotions are matters that may influence learning. Thus, they are important indicators when measuring effective teaching. Krathwohl et al. are credited with the development of the categorization of the affective domain of teaching.[12] The affective domain of teaching, again in ascending order, contains the objectives:

1. receiving,
2. responding,
3. valuing,
4. organization and
5. characterization by a value or value complex.

The receiving of knowledge refers to the students' willingness to attend class and do assignments. Responding is an objective that assesses the students' reactions to classroom activities and assignments. In other words, do they do their work and do they participate in class? Valuing refers to the student attaching worth to specific activities or knowledge. Organization pertains to the students' development of an internally consistent value system. The highest level of affective objectives is the characterization by a value or value complex. That is, that students use the values they have developed to guide their behaviors in everyday life.

The objectives found in the cognitive and the affective domains of teaching can be used to form the basis for several valuative criteria and processes. In fact, many presently used valuative techniques rely upon the cognitive and affective domains. For example, it is not uncommon for student survey instruments to have questions that obviously reflect specific cognitive or affective objectives.

THE ASSESSMENT OF TEACHING PERFORMANCE

How can the degree to which a professor exhibits effective teacher characteristics be measured? While it is generally accepted that teaching should be a major factor in faculty performance appraisals, conflict and controversy continue regarding the techniques and criteria used to measure teaching effectiveness. The purpose of this section is to discuss available means of assessing the quality of college teaching.

J. A. Centra has identified fifteen different methods of teaching evaluation used at North American colleges and universities:

1. systematic student ratings,
2. informal student opinions,
3. colleague ratings based on classroom visits,
4. colleague opinions based on "other" evidence,
5. student performance on exams,
6. peer evaluation of course outlines and exams,
7. department chairperson's evaluation,
8. dean's evaluation,
9. committee evaluation,
10. self-evaluation,
11. long-term follow-up of students' performance,
12. alumni opinions or ratings,
13. level of student enrollment in instructor's elective courses,
14. analysis of videotapes of classroom instruction and
15. participation in teaching improvement activities such as work-shops.[13]

In his survey of 453 department chairpersons at 134 colleges and universities, Centra found that chairpersons' evaluations, systematic student ratings and colleagues' opinions were the most frequently used and influential methods of evaluating teaching for promotion, tenure and salary purposes.[14]

The diversity of methods reported in Centra's study indicates that evaluation of teaching is therefore consistent across colleges and universities. Further, these institutions tend to rely on least-cost methods. Accordingly, he finds that most valuative schemes rely on internal resources and students. Even though Centra states that the department chairs surveyed reported that the three valuative techniques most often employed were the most "important" methods, there is little evidence concerning why these methods are important. Convenience and resource constraints could be factors easily as important as the reliability and/or validity of the processes employed. The relative importance of these factors is an empirical question that can only be answered on the basis of objective evidence.

The methods of the evaluation of instruction can be categorized into four groups by the source of the appraisal: self-evaluation, student evaluation, colleague/administrative appraisal and external assessment. Each of these categories will be examined in the following section.

SELF-EVALUATION

Self-evaluation of instruction is based on subjective evaluation of classroom performance by the individual professor. This method is sometimes augmented by the use of student questionnaires that are submitted directly to the professor who is not required to share their results with administration or colleagues.

Self-evaluation is rarely used as basis for personnel decisions. The reason that self-evaluation is rarely used for personnel decisions is the obvious potential lack of objectivity inherent in such a process. Self-evaluation, however, can be a useful technique when used in conjunction with administrator/colleague observations or student surveys to determine if the evaluatee's perceptions of his or her classroom performance are consistent with those of other potentially more objective observers. Differences in perceptions can often be used to identify weaknesses and strengths in teaching. The identification can then be used to improve instructional effectiveness. Beyond self-improvement, the self-evaluation process is of little value.

STUDENT EVALUATION OF INSTRUCTION

Student questionnaires have been the subject of the preponderance of research concerning teaching evaluation. Much has been written concerning the validity, utility and reliability of student assessments of instruction. In addition, student questionnaires are the most controversial of the methods of teaching assessment, even though the method is the most widely utilized in colleges and universities.[15]

Questionnaire Construction

The student evaluation process relies on questionnaires administered to students, commonly toward the end of a course. There are numerous questionnaires that have been developed and utilized for the purpose of obtaining student perceptions of the instruction they received. One researcher estimates that there are as many as several thousand different questionnaires currently used, and that few, if any, generalities can be offered concerning their construction.[16]

There are several questionnaires that have been validated and tested for reliability. Several contain items that were systematically selected to measure a wide variety of the dimensions of teaching for which student input may be appropriate. There are others that ask numerous general questions that may be difficult for students to interpret, may be inappropriate to ask students or may not be valid measures of teaching effectiveness. It is not uncommon for departments to develop their own questionnaire, even though in many cases there is no member of the faculty with the expertise to do so. In other words, the questionnaires and the process used to construct the questionnaires run a wide range from the systematic, valid and reliable to the absurd.

For a student evaluation questionnaire to be valid and systematic, it should be based upon some weighted measures of the identified dimensions of quality teaching. The domains of instructional objectives may be as good a starting point for the examination of this question as is available. There are several elements of both the cognitive and affective domain for which students may be able to provide meaningful feedback to the instructor and to evaluators. For example, whether a course held their attention, whether the instructor held their interest, or whether the course/ instructor was boring is something students can logically judge. Notice, however, these are distinct questions within the affective domain. Whether an instructor appeared to be organized in his or her classroom presentation is also something a student can judge. Again, the question lies in the affective domain. Notice further that all of these questions are focused at the lower end of the affective domain.

Logic would suggest that the affective domain is a legitimate area of evaluation. As we move from the lowest to the highest level in the affective domain, however, the responses to questionnaire items associated with higher levels become less obvious to interpret. If students are asked to respond to the question, "The instructor integrated the concepts in this course with concepts elsewhere in the curriculum," a freshman taking a first-year economics course would have no logical basis for passing judgment. A final semester senior may be able to make such a judgment, but only if the course is in her/his major. This sample question appears to be focused on the second affective level, organization. Any response, however, would reveal little about the student's ability to integrate concepts. Such a question only provides some information about whether the professor could integrate material from his/her course with material in other courses. This may be an important qualitative aspect of instruction for certain courses in certain curricula, but irrelevant in others.

Overall assessment questions are commonly included in evaluation questionnaires. To ask a student whether, "overall this was an effective instructor," makes little sense if the remaining items provide specific evidence concerning specific dimensions of teaching. Weighted averages of the items on the questionnaire are a more logical method of determining the overall effectiveness of an instructor. The weights to be used for the averages should reflect the relative importance of the specific items to the overall quality of instruction. Perhaps the easiest weighting scheme would assign greater importance to an item the higher its associated level in either the cognitive or affective domain. Such a weighted average scheme of the multiple dimensions of teaching, rather than an "overall sex appeal" question, is less likely to be confounded with biasing influences. If a single measure is to be the sole criterion for assessing the quality of instruction, then the weighted average, which is reflective of the total evaluation, is more logical.

There are questions concerning the number of items appropriate to student evaluation questionnaires. The optimal number of items for a questionnaire has not been conclusively identified in the literature. Marlin suggests that questionnaires with over forty items are "best used" for diagnostic rather than personnel decision purposes.[17] The majority of the widely adopted questionnaires (i.e., IDEA from Kansas State University and SEEQ from the University of Southern California) examine multiple dimensions of teaching. In general a minimum of nine items is normally included in the widely adopted questionnaires, and that is probably the minimum that could be effectively used in personnel decisions.

Procedures for Administration of Questionnaires

Assuming that a valid, reliable and appropriate questionnaire is constructed, there are several procedural questions that should be resolved. There is controversy concerning how many students should be polled and when they should be polled during an academic term. There is also a question about how often the questionnaire should be administered.

Naturally, student questionnaire results should not be given to instructors until after the final grades have been assigned in the course. This eliminates any suspicion students may have about potential retaliation for their assessments of their instructors. The remaining procedural questions have not been subjected to close scrutiny in the literature. There are, however, several of these issues that must be addressed.

There is little objective evidence that suggests the best time during a course for student questionnaires to be administered. Logically, the later in the course the better so that students are permitted the longest observation time possible. Moreover, the long observation period is consistent with the purpose of the process.

Most universities use a sampling technique for the administration of student questionnaires. An instructor may be asked to provide student evaluation results once a year for one course if they are used for personnel decisions. If questionnaires are administered in every class every semester, several substantive risks are inherent. Students are known to become ambivalent if they are continually asked to fill out questionnaires, but they see no substantive improvement in instruction based upon their feedback.[18] The use of evaluations in every section of every course may also become intrusive and may be viewed simply as a waste of classroom time.

Data Contamination

The construction of an evaluation questionnaire and the establishment of a procedure used to gather assessment data are only two of the issues associated with student evaluations. There is a significant body of literature that reports that questionnaire data are biased as a matter of course. That is, student respondents are influenced in answering the items by factors that are not intended. There is significant disagreement concerning whether bias is present in the data.

There is evidence that supports the contention that student evaluations are positively correlated with the grades students expect in the course.[19] There are those, however, that argue that as learning increases so should student evaluations of instruction.[20] Theoretically, this argument is flawed. It is primarily the affective domain that is measured in most student evaluations; the cognitive domain is rarely represented by a large number of items on any student evaluation questionnaire.[21] To assert that positive evaluations are associated with greater learning requires the establishment of a link between the cognitive, not the affective, domain and evaluations. Hence, the criticism of the argument that student evaluations are biased because of the positive correlation between evaluations and expected grades confuses the affective with the cognitive domain and may suffer from misspecification. In any event, the amount of correlation between expected grades and student ratings of instructors has been relatively small in most studies.

There are numerous other factors that have been discovered at specific institutions to be correlated with student evaluations of instructors. Gender differences, whether courses were required, the class status of students, class size and numerous other factors have been identified that influence student evaluations at specific schools.[22] In general, students taking classes that are taught by a female, are large and are required rather than elective systematically rated their instructors lower on the evaluation form. In addition, as students become more senior in their program of study, they tend to rate their instructors more highly.

To the extent that biasing influences in student evaluation data may be present, there must be reliable methods employed to identify and control for any relevant biases. Several methods are commonly available for identifying and dealing with any observed biases. Most of these methods are commonly accessible statistical methods and are easily applied.[23]

Student evaluations of instruction are an important element of the effective evaluation of teaching. There is a significant, perhaps crucial, role for the student questionnaire in teaching assessment. It should be recognized, however, that substantive criticisms of the student evaluation process exist. A substantial body of evidence demonstrates that there is significant potential for erroneous conclusions to be drawn from this method of assessment unless the questionnaires are properly constructed, properly administered, and the results examined and controlled for any observed biases. One would be mistaken to believe that the student evaluation of instruction can stand on its own as the only valuative instrument. There simply are a great number of the dimensions of effective teaching that student evaluation is not well equipped to handle.

Students can provide a great deal of usable information about instructional effectiveness. Students, however, are students, not pedagogical experts or colleagues. Accordingly, there is a limit to what can be expected from survey instruments. If students are asked to comment on those elements of teaching that are within their ability to assess reasonably, then the questionnaire method can be an important element of a total program of instructional evaluation.

ADMINISTRATIVE/COLLEAGUE APPRAISAL

Faculty and administrators who are knowledgeable in the instructor's field and experienced in the classroom are sometimes thought to be qualified judges of teaching effectiveness. Such persons would appear to be qualified to assess the instructor's knowledge, selection of course objectives and appropriateness of assignments and exams. In addition to evaluating dimensions of effective classroom instruction, these peers can evaluate other aspects of teaching such as supervision of student research, involvement in teaching improvement activities, curriculum development, preparation of instructional materials and research by the instructor related to teaching. Means by which colleagues and administrators can accomplish their evaluations of teaching include classroom visitation, appraisal of course materials, analysis of videotapes, and interpretation of student ratings.

Classroom visitation is perhaps the most controversial of the collegial methods of teaching evaluation. Professors are frequently not receptive to classroom visits because they are sometimes considered demeaning to an individual's professional standing and an infringement upon academic freedom. Evidence on colleague ratings based upon classroom observation indicates that they tend to be less reliable and often more biased than student ratings of classroom instruction. J. A. Centra has found that these visitation ratings show less inter-rater reliability and a greater bias toward leniency than do student ratings. He concludes from such results that, under normal circumstances, colleague visitation ratings are not reliable enough to use for personnel decisions. Of course, the reliability of colleague visitation ratings could be improved by increasing the number of raters and/or giving the raters special training in classroom observation techniques. Each of these can be expensive in both faculty time and effort.[24]

Researchers at the University of Illinois agree with Centra about the bias toward greater leniency in visitation ratings. They found that almost all colleagues rate their peers as excellent or good instructors. In addition, they report that the relationship between observed instructor behavior and student learning is not very strong. Findings like these make the validity of colleague visitation ratings suspect, and cause researchers to conclude that colleague evaluation based on classroom visitation is more appropriate for faculty development purposes than for personnel decisions. Nonetheless, if visitation ratings are used for personnel decisions, it is recommended that several colleagues each make visits to a given class during a single term in order to ensure adequate representation. In addition, the areas to be evaluated during the visitation should be agreed upon in advance.[25] Colleagues can provide valuable, reliable and valid assessments of course materials such as examinations, syllabi and instructional media.[26] Colleagues and administrators may be effective evaluators in teaching activities outside of the classroom such as curriculum development and participation in teaching improvement activities. The preponderance of research in this area has focused on graduate student supervision. There is certainly a need for further research in colleague appraisal.[27] It can be safely concluded, however, that colleague assessments can be used to assess instructional materials.

Testing

Cognitive testing can be both an external and colleague/administrator assessment technique. If there are standardized tests in a specific academic discipline developed by a professional organization, university or other external entity, then cognitive testing is probably more appropriately classified as external evaluation. It does no great violence, however, to include all cognitive testing in this section.

Cognitive testing is being used in many academic institutions. In economics, instructors may avail themselves of standardized tests of the mastery of economic principles, accompanied by nationally normed data that can be readily used for comparisons. In some cases, departments develop standardized tests for introductory and survey courses to assure that the course content is being given adequate attention by all faculty members teaching those courses. Where such cognitive tests exist, several of the elements of the cognitive domain can readily be assessed by pre- and post-testing students to determine the learning they accomplished in any specific class.

If departmental exams are developed and used, they should be subjected to rigorous validation and reliability tests to ensure that the content of the exams is appropriate to the purpose and that the question items are properly constructed. It may be wise to have outside experts in the academic area review the examinations to ensure that the content is appropriate. Testing experts could review the construction of the test items to assure their quality.

Cognitive testing may be the only reasonable way in which to evaluate instructional performance in many of the cognitive domain levels. Even though its use is not yet widespread outside of economics, cognitive testing is worthy of careful consideration for inclusion in a total assessment program.

EXTERNAL EVALUATION

The use of external evaluators is still relatively rare for teaching effectiveness. It is not uncommon to have outside experts evaluate a professor's research output, but it is less common to use outside experts to evaluate a professor's classroom performance. Nevertheless, there is some movement toward assessment using videotaped classroom lectures sent to outside experts in educational pedagogy or in the academic field. Little or no empirical evidence exists that permits conclusions to be drawn concerning any possible biases and the reliability of such external assessments. The use of external experts may provide a remedy for leniency bias of collegial evaluations because the experts are not colleagues (i.e., employed by the same university) of the individual they are being asked to evaluate.

Viewing syllabi and other course materials, outside experts in a faculty member's field can provide valuable information concerning course organization and content in much the same manner as colleagues or administrators. Because the external evaluator is not a member of the same faculty as the person being evaluated, (s)he will not have personal loyalties, political connections or fear of possible recrimination emanating from a negative evaluation. Thus, on face, external evaluation offers the possibility of more valid and reliable assessments. The use of outside experts could also supplement any expertise that may presently exist within a given faculty, thereby providing more resources for instructional development and effective personnel decision making. Outside expert evaluation is, therefore, an obvious source of improved instructional evaluation.

There are other sources of external feedback. Students become alumni. Once graduated, they may be regarded as external sources of valuative comments. Alumni can be surveyed to determine if specific faculty members provided exceptional instruction (either good or bad). Alumni surveys have several benefits. The most obvious is that the alumni may have several years of work experience, and thus, time to reflect on their educational experience. Consequently, alumni may have a unique perspective on certain of the affective and cognitive domain factors that were not readily apparent when they were students. They are, after all, the end-users of the education they received. Again, there has been very little research on alumni surveys, so they should be used with great caution.

TOTAL TEACHING ASSESSMENT

Ethical appraisal requires as complete an assessment of teaching performance as resources will permit. The preceding discussion of teaching evaluation demonstrates that there are several methods of instructional assessment, all with strengths and weaknesses. Logic suggests that if the appraisal of teaching performance is to be effective it must employ several sources of reliable and valid data. This should occur in a systematic and logical system. Student surveys used with peer visitations to classrooms and expert assessments of examinations and syllabi provide an interlocking coverage of pedagogical and cognitive teaching activities. If consistent evidence is adduced through this system, corroboration of evidence between the measurement devices is also likely.

Cognitive testing may also be a viable alternative for instructional assessment of the cognitive domain in many disciplines. It may also be difficult to apply in several areas, such as the fine arts or English composition. The cognitive issues of college instruction are of particular interest. It is expected that professors with Ph.D.s will know their fields and have kept current so that their courses will be up-to-date. An intellectually active faculty member who has consistently contributed to her or his discipline is probably not going to fail in the cognitive domain, as long as the intellectual contributions of the professor's research program are relevant to her/his instructional responsibilities. Too often, however, there are cognitive problems. Those without the necessary academic credentials and intellectual activity may not be competent to teach in the areas in which they are assigned. Those faculty members who are working on cutting-edge research of an advanced nature may not be able to bring an introductory course to the level normally expected. Simply assuming that an instructor performs adequately in the cognitive domain is ill-advised. Evaluation of his/her competence in this area should be a portion of the total teaching assessment program.

It is also worth mentioning that this portion of the assessment may be useful in individual programs of professional improvement, rather than simply to feed the personnel decision process. Particularly, intrinsically motivated teachers will want the opportunity to use the evidence gathered in the teaching assessment to improve their teaching. Extrinsically motivated individuals may need to see the connection of the teaching assessment evidence and the rewards and punishment system before self-assessment and improvement activities are undertaken.

SUMMARY AND CONCLUSIONS

There are various forms of university teaching and different dimensions of teaching effectiveness. With all of the possible combinations of teaching types and effective teaching characteristics, university teaching is clearly a complex activity that requires a multifaceted system of evaluation. Of course, it is unnecessary to include all types of teaching, dimensions of effectiveness and valuative methods in any one system. Instead, it is recommended that the selection of the components for a unit's teaching evaluation system be guided by the factors identified as being associated with effective teaching. The factors identified should be determined by the institution's mission, the purpose of the evaluation (i.e., personnel decisions or faculty development) and available evidence concerning the reliability and validity of evaluation techniques.

NOTES

1. P. Seldin, *Successful Faculty Evaluation Programs* (Crugers, N.Y.: Coventry Press), 1980, p. 18.

2. W. E. Cashin, *IDEA Paper No. 20: A Summary of Research* (Manhattan: Kansas State University, Center for Faculty Evaluation and Development), 1988.

3. Numerous studies are reported that have cast doubt as to the validity of student evaluations of instruction. For example, see M. Rodin and B. Rodin, "Student Evaluation of Teachers," *Journal of Economic Education* (Fall 1973), pp. 5–9; and D. A. Dilts, "A Statistical Interpretation of Student Evaluation Feedback," *Journal of Economic Education* (Spring 1980), pp. 10–15.

4. P. Seldin, *Changing Practices in Faculty Evaluation* (San Francisco: Jossey-Bass), 1984, p. 25.

5. K. A. Feldman, "The Superior College Teacher From the Students' View," *Research in Higher Education*, vol. 5 (1976), pp. 277–86.

6. J. W. Marlin and J. F. Niss, "Student Evaluation of Teachers: Evidence of the Western Illinois Experiment." Center for Business and Economic Research, Western Illinois University, Working Paper 1979–15, June 1979.

7. P. Saunders and W. B. Walstad, *The Principles of Economics Course. A Handbook for Instructors* (New York: McGraw-Hill Book Company), 1990, p. 63.

8. B. F. Skinner, *The Technology of Teaching* (New York: Appleton-Century-Crofts), 1968.

9. J. S. Brunner, *Toward a Theory of Instruction* (Cambridge: Belknap Press), 1966.

10. R. M. Cagne, *The Conditions of Learning and the Theory of Instruction*, 4th ed. (New York: Holt, Rinehart and Winston), 1985.

11. This array of cognitive objectives is commonly called "Bloom's Taxonomy" after the educator who first identified it. See N. F. Gronlund, *Stating Instructional Objectives for Classroom Instruction* (New York: Macmillan Publishing Company), 1985, for further discussion.

12. Ibid.

13. J. A. Centra, *How Universities Evaluate Faculty Performance: A Survey of Department Heads*, GREB Research Report No. 75-5bR (Princeton, N.J.: Educational Testing Service), 1977.

14. Ibid.

15. H. G. Murray, *Evaluating University Teaching: A Review of Research* (Toronto: Ontario Confederation of University Faculty Associations), 1980, p. 3.

16. J. W. Marlin, "Student Evaluations of Instruction: Decipher the Message," in P. Saunders and W. B. Walstad, *The Principles of Economics Course. A Handbook for Instructors* (New York: McGraw-Hill Book Company), 1990, p. 242.

17. Ibid.

18. Marlin, p. 238.

19. See, for example, Hamid Zangenehzadeh, "Grade Inflation: A Way Out,"

Journal of Economic Education, vol. 19 (Summer 1988), pp. 217–26; and V. W. Voeks and G. M. French, "Are Student Ratings of Teachers Affected by Grades?," *Journal of Higher Education* (June 1960), pp. 330–34.

20. Marlin, p. 244.

21. See M. E. Wetzstein, J. M. Broder and G. Wilson, "Bayesian Inference and Student Evaluation of Teachers and Courses," *Journal of Economic Education* (Winter 1984), pp. 40–45.

22. For example, see D. A. Dilts, "A Statistical Interpretation of Student Evaluation Feedback," *Journal of Economic Education* (Spring 1980), pp. 10–15; A. C. Kelley, "Uses and Abuses of Course Evaluations as Measures of Educational Output," *Journal of Economic Education* (Fall 1972), pp. 13–18; and F. Costin, W. T. Greenough and R. J. Menges, "Student Ratings of College Teaching: Reliability, Validity, and Usefulness," *Review of Educational Research*, vol. 11 (1971), pp. 511–35, for further discussion of this topic.

23. For example, see Dilts (1980); and Zangenehzadeh (1988).

24. J. A. Centra, "Colleagues as Raters of Classroom Instruction," *Journal of Higher Education*, vol. 46 (1975), pp. 327–37.

25. L. A. Braskamp, D. C. Brandenbury and J. C. Ory, *Evaluating Teaching Effectiveness: A Practical Guide* (Beverly Hills: Sage Publications, Inc.), 1984, p. 66.

26. J. A. Kulik and W. J. McKeachie, "The Evaluation of Teachers in Higher Education," in F. N. Kerlinger (ed.), *Review of Research in Education*, vol. 3 (Itasca, Ill.: Peacock Publishers), 1975, p. 236.

27. E. A. Rugg and R. C. Norris, "Student Ratings of Individualized Faculty Supervision: Description and Evaluation," *American Educational Research Journal*, vol. 12 (1975), pp. 41–53.

Chapter 6

The Evaluation of Research

Over the past several decades, the efforts of college and university professors have been increasingly devoted to research. Not only is the increased emphasis evident at major campuses with traditions of research excellence, but at emerging institutions which aspire to recognition as self-contained, comprehensive universities. Even many liberal arts colleges have emphasized scholarly activity as a means of faculty development.[1] The greater weight assigned to research in personnel evaluations reflects the trend and has led to increased scrutiny of methods by which scholarly productivity is measured. A review of the proposed measures and their relative strengths forms the body of this chapter.

As argued earlier, competence in research must be demonstrated by publication in order to ensure the responsiveness of a faculty member to critical review. Publication is also necessary to show one's willingness and ability to contribute to his/her discipline. In this light, research and consequent publications can be expected to have at least two salutary effects on an administrative unit:

1. They aid in the professional development of the faculty. That is, research contributes to the intellectual vitality of a department. Also, to the extent that research supports instructional efforts, it improves the quality of teaching.
2. They bring external recognition to a department or school. Many studies have linked prestige of a department to the research

productivity of its faculty or of the students that it graduates. More concretely, accrediting bodies frequently assess the level of publication activity and its dispersion within a department or school.[2]

In most departments, both internal and external benefits of research are present to varying degrees. The precise mix of benefits in large part determines the criteria by which it is evaluated. For example, at major universities where external recognition of research is paramount, book reviews or other service publications alone will carry little weight. Conversely, at liberal arts colleges, such publications may be viewed as evidence that a faculty member is keeping up with developments in his/her field and, therefore, receive much greater consideration. Clearly then, any of the evaluative methods reviewed must be adapted to the unique missions of a department or school.

Seemingly, a professor's research activity is more easily evaluated than his/her teaching. Evaluation of research should be easier because measures of the outputs of the research process (i.e., publications) are readily available. While an evaluator can view purported outputs, translation of those identifiable outputs into an evaluation is by no means straightforward. There are several questions that require examination:

1. How does one assess the relative value of one type of publication against another? For example, how does one weight the publication of a book vis-à-vis journal articles?
2. Can one assess the quality of the medium in which a publication appears? For example, can one rank journals by quality?
3. Can one measure the impact of a work more directly than by ascertaining the quality of the medium in which it appears?

Through the work of others and through our own analysis, we hope to provide some guidelines for the assessment of research in personnel actions.

METHODS OF EVALUATION

Given that the measure of research activity is publication, the issue remains of what criteria to use in evaluating a record of publications. While the literature gives no definitive answers, it does enumerate a number of criteria and weigh the relative strengths of each.

Simple Counts

Perhaps the simplest method of evaluating research is to rank faculty by a quantity index. If publication is the objective of research, then the more ideas of an individual that his peers judge to have merit, the more productive the individual. By judging over some period of time, one can construct a rough measure of relative productivity by judging the rate at which different faculty members in a discipline are publishing.

The primary objection to ranking in this manner is that quantity measures alone fail to take into account the quality of the work being published. Even if one establishes some minimum standard of quality that a publication must meet in order to "count" in the quantity index, once the threshold requirement is met, all publications are identical. For example, an article in the most prestigious journal in a discipline might carry the same weight as an article in a regional journal under this method of ranking. Because the quality of an individual's contribution is arguably at least as important as the quantity in bringing that individual recognition,[3] most researchers and administrators believe that correction for quality is necessary.[4]

Weighted Indices

The issue becomes how best to measure quality. One approach that has been commonly taken measures the quality of the medium in which a work is published. By grouping and classifying possible outlets for publication and by establishing weights for each class of publication, one may compute an index of research productivity as the weighted sum of an individual's output during a given period of time. For example, suppose that a department determined that publication in one of the most prestigious journals in the discipline (those journals enumerated by the department) was worth ten points per article, while publication in a less prestigious (perhaps regional) journal might be worth only half that number of points, five points per article. A trade publication or a book review might be worth one point per publication. Further, suppose that in a year, an individual in the department published one article in the most prestigious journal in the field, two in less prestigious journals and three in trade publications. Consequently, the individual would have earned twenty-three research points for the year ($[1 \times 10] + [2 \times 5] + [3 \times 1]$). The score could be compared against those of others in determining salary increments, or against some absolute standard in determining worthiness for promotion or tenure. Although the basic framework will remain the same, specific

levels of performance will differ from department to department according
to mission.

Establishing a rating system for journals and other media only removes
the issue of quality of research to another level. That is, even if one accepts
that the quality of research can be measured in the media (especially
journals) in which a faculty member publishes, how should the quality of
media be ascertained? Among the references listed at the end of the chapter
are numerous studies that rank journals within various fields of study. The
studies have used several different methods to accomplish the ranking.
Again, there is no best method, but a critical review points to the strengths
and weaknesses of each.

The most prevalent method of ranking journals is by direct survey of
researchers or administrators. If the sampling for a survey is done properly,
then the rankings obtained represent the consensus view of the prestige of
the journals. The positive evaluation of an individual's work by others
may aid both the individual and his/her department in obtaining financial
resources. Abbott and Barlow[5] report a positive correlation between
resources and prestige, mediated by controls for department functions such
as research.[6] While this method of establishing quality is based on the
subjective judgment of individuals, it may accurately reflect that research
which will bring external recognition and prestige to the individual investigator and, by extension, to his/her department.

There are weaknesses inherent in quality rankings of journals established by survey. Because of the proliferation of journals in many
disciplines, faculty in those disciplines no longer have firsthand knowledge
of many of the journals. Imperfect knowledge renders suspect rankings based
on perception or reputation. For example, in their study ranking economics
journals, Hawkins, Ritter and Walter included the names of two fictitious
journals in their survey form.[7] For each bogus journal, slightly less than
twenty percent of the 111 economists responding claimed familiarity with
that journal. One of the journals, with the appropriate acronym J.E.S.T.,
was ranked twenty-fourth in quality from a list of eighty-seven journals
by those claiming familiarity. The authors also constructed a prestige
index, calculated by measuring the mean ranking multiplied by the percentage claiming familiarity. Using the index, J.E.S.T. was ranked ahead
of twenty-six existing journals. That a nonexistent journal could be ranked
higher than many existing journals casts doubt upon the validity of the
survey measures. The difficulty with surveys is that one cannot observe
the traits of journals that respondents use to establish rankings, and
therefore, one cannot assess the extent to which the rankings actually
measure quality.

Another way to evaluate the quality of a journal is to examine the number of citations that the journal receives in other media. Most commonly, studies have observed the frequency with which the journal is cited in other journals,[8] although Skeels and Taylor measure the frequency with which journals are cited on graduate reading lists.[9] The logic of these measures is that the more prestigious a journal the more widely it is known and the more frequently it is cited. Thus, frequency of citation measures both the visibility of a journal and the recognition that it receives.

In a survey of economics journals, Laband finds that there was wide variation in the number of citations received by articles in the same journal.[10] He concludes that measuring citations to infer the quality of journals is misleading. Because a disproportionate share of the citations that a journal receives comes from a relatively small percentage of its constituent articles, Laband suggests that journals are relatively close substitutes, but authors and articles are not. As he states: "Economists will read a good article, regardless of where it appears." Because, as evidenced by the disparity in citation counts, the quality of articles appearing in a given journal is highly variable, the use of citation counts to establish the quality of a journal and, by extension, the quality of a given article is an imperfect measure.

Others have attempted to measure journal quality using objective characteristics of the journals. Moore,[11] for example, orders economics journals by measuring the percentage of articles contributed from prestigious departments (where the prestige of departments is determined by American Council on Education evaluations).[12] Unfortunately, one cannot assess whether it is the departments that lend prestige to the journal, or the reverse. That is, there is a simultaneity problem. Anderson and Goldstein, in a study of biomedical journals, suggest that several objective criteria, such as comprehensive statements of editorial policy and refereeing criteria, in addition to frequency of citation by other journals, all correlate with a journal's quality.[13]

Regardless of how the index is constructed, the use of a journal quality index to determine research quality has shortcomings. In particular, the way in which the indices are customarily applied assumes that all articles published in the same journal are of equal quality and, therefore, receive equal weight. As noted above, Laband finds, however, that articles published in the same journal often receive very different degrees of recognition (as measured by frequency of citation).[14] If the differential recognition indeed reflects differential quality, then assigning the same weight to all articles published in the same journal may provide only a rough measure of quality of research.

Another issue that arises in a system where publications are weighted according to the media in which they are published is how to rate different types of publications. Specifically, what is the relative weight that should be attached to a book when compared with an article. Most of the evidence of how book publication is regarded comes implicitly when authors, for various reasons, have constructed productivity indices. The relative weights given books and articles, then, form some assessment of the importance of each type of publication in overall research productivity. Unfortunately, there is wide divergence in authors' opinions about the relative weights. Meltzer[15] and Manis[16] equate writing an article with writing a chapter in a book. Because he found that the average book in the social sciences had eighteen chapters, Manis weighted authorship of a book as equivalent to the publication of eighteen articles. Crane[17] equates book authorship to authorship of four journal articles, while Jauch and Glueck, in their productivity index, merely added the number of books to the number of papers, implying an equivalence between one book and one paper.[18] All of these weights are subjectively determined and represent the appraisals of the authors concerned rather than any general consensus.

One means to assess general attitudes about the relative weight that should be given to book publication is by looking at models of salary determination. For instance, Katz, in a study of salary determination in eleven departments at a major, public university during the 1969–1970 academic year, found that, after controlling for many variables, a first book by a professor added $451 in salary.[19] On the other hand, an ordinary (as opposed to excellent) article yielded a $111 average increase in salary if the professor had published no more than eight articles previously. Then, for a person at the beginning of an academic career (with no book or articles published), one book would equate to approximately four ordinary journal articles.

Aside from a lack of generality engendered by sampling only at one university, other factors prevent a straightforward interpretation of the results. The relationships between articles and salary and between books and salary is nonlinear. Depending upon the relative number of books and articles already published, the worth of a book in terms of article equivalents will change. From Katz's figures, for an individual who has published numerous articles (more than thirty-eight) but no books, the first book would be worth approximately eight journal articles (rather than the four if the individual had published no articles).[20]

Tuckman, Gapinski and Hagemann test a model similar to Katz's, but with the sample extended to include data at 301 institutions across a broad range of departments for the 1972–1973 academic year.[21] Also, they divide the sample into disciplines (social sciences, liberal arts, mathematics-engineering, biological sciences and physical sciences). Their results indicate much lower relative rewards for book publishing in general, with the rewards differing widely among the disciplines. For the case of a faculty member with no prior publications, a first book is worth at most one article (in the social sciences) while it on average is shown to be negatively related to salary in the biological sciences. The negative relationship in the biological sciences is not statistically significant, however. Until consistency of results can be found between different universities or different disciplines over time, one can make few general statements about the relative rewards to book publishing.

Employing a weighted index to measure research productivity implies that the administrative unit must decide how to remunerate coauthorship. There are two methods commonly employed in the construction of productivity indices. The first method weights an article or book the same, regardless of the number of authors. The number of books and articles on which an individual is listed as author determines the ranking in the productivity index.[22] An individual who published ten coauthored articles would be viewed as equally productive as an individual, with a like number of articles, who was the sole author of each. The second method, conversely, assigns a proportionate weight to each author.[23] Thus, a faculty member who published an article of which he was the sole author would receive full credit for that article, while an individual who was one of n authors of an article would receive only $1/nth$ the credit. The two methods represent limiting cases. In the evaluation of personnel, intermediate methods that reflect the unique values of an academic institution are, of course, practicable. More generally, there is no research to indicate either general academic or disciplinary norms in this matter. The best that may be deduced is that the weighting system for coauthorship adopted by a school or department will create incentives likely to affect patterns of publication within that unit. A method of evaluation that gives equal weight to single authorship and coauthorship will likely result in much more joint research effort within a unit than a method that gives coauthorship much less weight. In choosing a weighting system, one must confront issues of both incentives created and equity.

Citation Counts

Rather than evaluating research by evaluating the medium in which the research is published, a number of authors have suggested that the contribution made by a faculty member's research be directly assessed by counting the number of citations made to that person's work. With the advent of citation indexes in most disciplines, the task has been made immeasurably easier. While the indexes do not measure every possible source of citation, they do represent the vast preponderance of significant journals in a given field. With some qualification, the number of citations to a given work in the indexes measures the degree to which the work has been recognized within a discipline and the degree to which it has proved influential.[24]

Perhaps the most glaring weakness of citation counts to measure the recognition a work or group of works has received is the fact that some citations, far from being complimentary, can be quite unfavorable. A work cited many times unfavorably does not bring credit to the author or his/her institution of employment. Stigler and Friedland analyze both the frequency of favorable citation and unfavorable citation in their study of dominant economics scholars in the period from 1950 to 1968.[25] As well, Stigler and Friedland found that certain authors received the great majority of their favorable citations from only a few other authors. Even though recognition is desirable, if numerous citations come from only a few sources, then the citation count may well overstate the significance of the work.

Smith and Fiedler point out that citation counts provide evidence of quality and recognition only over an extended period of time.[26] Some works are recognized only long after their publication. Although Cole and Cole cite evidence that over two-thirds of citations to published physics articles occur within five years of publication, even this time frame may be inadequate to fairly evaluate the dossier of a junior professor approaching tenure six years after the beginning of his career.[27] Smith and Fiedler also note the tendency of authors to cite well-known authorities, rather than unknown researchers when a choice of sources exists. The tendency exists because the citation of the authority will lend greater credence to the research in question. For both reasons, citation counts can be misleading indicators of the quality of a faculty member's research.

COMPARISON OF EVALUATION METHODS

Each proposed measure for evaluation of research has both strengths and weaknesses. There have been several studies whose results can be used to compare the methods. While the evidence does not point to a uniform conclusion, several themes emerge that are instructive.

Cole and Cole, in a survey of university physicists, provide the first piece of information.[28] They seek to determine whether the quantity or the quality of a scientist's work contributes more to its recognition. Three separate measures of recognition are used. First, from their survey, the authors found that there were forty-two awards that were known to at least twenty percent of the physicists surveyed. Accordingly, the number of times that a faculty member received one of these awards was a measure of that person's eminence. Because affiliation with top-ranked departments also conveys prestige to an individual, the rank (taken from Cartter) of the department employing that individual constituted the second measure of recognition.[29] Finally, Cole and Cole surveyed the percentage of colleagues familiar with a given individual's work. The percentage represents the scope of a scientist's reputation and formed the third measure of recognition. As independent variables, the authors measured the total number of papers published and the number of papers per year as indices of quantity of output. As well, they used a weighted citation index as indicative of the quality of that research. In examining the correlations between the measures of recognition and the measures of quantity and of quality, Cole and Cole found that the quality measure was uniformly more highly correlated with the recognition measures than were either of the quantity measures. They take that as evidence that, at least in physics, quality of work is more highly valued than quantity of research. In fact, for those scientists who produced high quality work, the actual quantity of research that they published seemed to have virtually no effect on their probability of winning at least one of the prestigious awards.

The results of the Cole and Cole study must be qualified. One reason for caution is that, as Cole and Cole admit, theirs is a stratified sample which overrepresents eminent scientists. The results, therefore, explain the determinants of recognition within that group only. The restricted nature of the sample limits the applicability of the results to the design of incentive schemes at major research universities for whom external recognition described in the study is of paramount consideration.

If the results of Cole and Cole hold in general, the implication is that a faculty member's research should be judged primarily by the number of citations because that is how he is judged within his/her discipline. Smith and Fiedler cite several additional studies that, like Cole and Cole, establish the relationship between citation counts and eminence at major research universities.[30] Smith and Fiedler contend that this demonstrated relationship makes citation counts a conceptually sounder method of evaluating research than quality-weighted publication indices.

Jauch and Glueck take a different approach and, not surprisingly, obtain different results.[31] They surveyed eighty-six faculty members in twenty-three departments at the University of Missouri-Columbia during the 1970 academic year. The authors' rank ordered the faculty according to eleven dimensions of research performance cited in previous research. The measures fell into three categories: quantity measures, quality measures and eminence measures. Moreover, all of them were found to be interrelated. Jauch and Glueck propose that each of the measures contributes, to some degree, to research productivity. To form an overall indicator of research performance, they averaged the rank orders across all eleven dimensions. Acknowledging that measuring research performance along eleven dimensions would be cumbersome at best, the authors seek a simpler measure by examining the correlation of the component indices with the composite index and by examining the correlation of combinations of indices with the composite index. They found that the highest correlation between the composite index and a single index was with the number of papers, books and technical reports published (i.e., the number of publications). When they considered combinations of indices, the highest correlation was with the sum of the number of papers published and refereed. Additional variables, including both journal quality index and number of citations, did not improve the correlation with the composite index. The inference that Jauch and Glueck draw is that, as far as their sample was concerned, simple quantitative measures of research output were sufficient to judge the overall research performance of faculty.

Jauch and Glueck go further, however. They sent questionnaires to the eighty-six faculty and to the twenty-three heads of the departments from which the faculty were sampled. The questionnaires revealed that both the department heads and the faculty believed that quality measures were superior to simple counts in judging research performance. Although both journal quality indices and number of citations were judged superior to simple counts, the preferred measure of performance was peer evaluation. Because people act on what they believe to be true, Jauch and Glueck suggest that the attitudes of faculty and administrators must be taken into account. They conclude that a quality-weighted publication index may represent the best compromise solution. Such an index was only slightly less correlated with the composite index than was a simple count of publications, and quality weighting has the virtue of consistency with academic attitudes (and, therefore, is more likely to engender faculty support).

It is not surprising that those studies advocating use of citation measures drew inference from samples of faculty who were already eminent, and consequently worked at prestigious, research-oriented universities.[32] Jauch and Glueck, however, conducted their study entirely at the University of Missouri-Columbia.[33] While Missouri is a major state university, a perusal of the departmental rankings of Roose and Anderson, carried out several years before the Jauch and Glueck survey, reveals that Missouri was not ranked among the top twenty departments (although frequently in the top fifty departments) in quality of graduate faculty in any rated discipline.[34] The fact that the number of citations that a faculty member received was relatively less correlated than simple quantity measures to almost any other measure of research productivity may reflect the nature of the sample. While citations and other forms of external recognition may be highly correlated among the most eminent researchers at the top-ranked universities, the correlation may be much lower at lower-ranked institutions. This view is corroborated by Crane[35] and Cole and Cole.[36] Employing different measures of research productivity, both studies found that not only were faculty at lower-ranked universities less likely to achieve high research productivity, but they were less likely to gain recognition than faculty at higher-ranked universities who had been equally productive. Thus, external recognition and research productivity (whether measured using Crane's modified publication counts or Cole and Cole's citation counts) are less closely tied at less highly ranked universities. If external recognition of research is unlikely, then the purpose that research fulfills at lower-ranked universities is primarily internal. That is, research may be sanctioned primarily for the professional development of the resident faculty.

The question remains as to what generalizations may be drawn from the studies comparing methods of research evaluation. What is evident from the majority of work in the field is the close association of citation counts and external recognition among eminent faculty. On a conceptual basis as well, if external recognition is the primary objective of, and consequently, the primary means by which research is to be evaluated, then the number of citations that a faculty member's research receives is the optimal method. On the other hand, if the primary goal of research within an academic unit is the professional development of its faculty, and if external recognition beyond that required by accrediting agencies is not as important, then citation counts become less critical in evaluating research. In that case, quality-weighted publication indices may replace citation counts as the method of choice. More easily calculated and interpreted, quality-weighted publication indices also have the advantage of setting definite, objective standards for evaluation. A faculty member can ascertain in a straightforward manner how his/her record matches against those standards required for tenure or for promotion to any rank.

Another consideration that arises in the comparison of methods of evaluating research is the time frame over which the measures are applied.

While simple publication counts and quality-weighted publication indices both provide contemporaneous evaluation of a faculty member's research performance, citation counts provide evidence of external recognition only several years after the publication of a work. Consequently, citation counts are better than the other two measures for judging the significance of an individual's record only over an extended period of time. Citation measures may not gauge properly the significance of the publications of a candidate for tenure, and consequent promotion to associate professor, because the probationary period is short. On the other hand, citation measures are more appropriate in cases of promotion to full professor where time constraints are less restricting.

SUMMARY AND CONCLUSIONS

In summary, each measure of research productivity examined here has both strengths and weaknesses. The choice of measure, or combination of measures, employed should be dependent upon the purpose of research within an academic unit and the nature of the personnel action undertaken. Within that unit, if the primary objective of research is external recognition, then the best indicator of that recognition is number of citations. If faculty development is the principal purpose that research serves, then simple publication counts or quality-weighted indices have much to commend them. These measures set objective standards that are, at minimum, positively correlated with any other measure of research productivity and that set objective standards against which faculty can gauge their performance at any point in time. In addition, because publication and citation are not simultaneous, citation counts indicate external recognition only over some extended period. Conversely, the simple counts or quality-weighted indices give credit immediately at publication. Only where the period of evaluation is sufficiently long will citation measures accurately gauge performance.

NOTES

1. F. S. Weaver, "Scholarship and Teaching," *Educational Record* (Winter 1989), pp. 54–58.

2. Among many possible examples, see P. E. Graves, J. R. Marchand and R. Thompson, "Economics Department Rankings: Research Incentives, Constraints, Efficiency," *American Economic Review* (December 1982), pp. 1131–41; W. O. Hagstrom, "Inputs, Outputs, and the Prestige of University Science Departments," *Sociology of Education* (Fall 1971), pp. 375–97; T. D. Hogan, "Rankings of Ph.D. Programs in Economics and the Relative Publishing Perfor-

mance of their Ph.D.s: The Experience of the 1960's," *Western Economic Journal* (1973), pp. 429–50; and J. J. Siegfried, "The Publishing of Economic Papers and Its Impact on Graduate Faculty Ratings," *Journal of Economic Literature* (March 1972), pp. 31–49.

3. S. Cole and J. R. Cole, "Scientific Output and Recognition: A Study in the Operation of the Reward System in Science," *American Sociological Review* (June 1967), pp. 377–90.

4. For documentation, see L. R. Jauch and W. F. Glueck, "Evaluation of University Professors' Research Performance," *Management Science* (September 1975), pp. 66–75; and R. Smith and F. E. Fiedler, "The Measurement of Scholarly Work: A Critical Review of the Literature," *Educational Record* (Summer 1971), pp. 225–32.

5. W. F. Abbott and H. M. Barlow, "Stratification Theory and Organizational Rank: Resources, Functions, and Organizational Prestige in American Universities," *Pacific Sociological Review* (October 1972), pp. 401–24.

6. It should be noted, however, that they suggest that the causality runs from resources to prestige rather than from prestige to resources. The two hypotheses are empirically indistinguishable in cross-section studies.

7. R. G. Hawkins, L. S. Ritter and I. Walter, "What Economists Think of Their Journals," *Journal of Political Economy* (July/August 1973), pp. 1017–32.

8. Several of these studies are: B. B. Billings and G. J. Viksnins, "The Relative Quality of Economics Journals: An Alternative Rating System," *Western Economic Journal* (December 1972), pp. 467–69; W. C. Bush, P. W. Hamelman and R. J. Staaf, "A Quality Index for Economics Journals," *Review of Economics and Statistics* (February 1974), pp. 123–25; and S. J. Liebowitz and J. P. Palmer, "Assessing the Relative Impacts of Economics Journals," *Journal of Economic Literature* (March 1984), pp. 77–88.

9. J. W. Skeels and R. A. Taylor, "The Relative Quality of Economics Journals: An Alternative Rating System," *Western Economic Journal* (December 1972), pp. 470–73.

10. D. N. Laband, "Article Popularity," *Economic Inquiry* (January 1986), pp. 173–80.

11. W. J. Moore, "The Relative Quality of Economics Journals: A Suggested Rating System," *Western Economics Journal* (June 1972), pp. 156–69.

12. K. D. Roose and C. J. Anderson, *A Rating of Graduate Programs* (Washington, D.C.: American Council on Education), 1970.

13. P. J. Anderson and R. K. Goldstein, "Criteria of Journal Quality," *Journal of Research Communication Studies* (1981), pp. 99–110.

14. Laband, pp. 177–79.

15. B. N. Meltzer, "The Productivity of Social Scientists," *American Journal of Sociology* (July 1949), pp. 25–29.

16. J. G. Manis, "Some Academic Influences upon Publication Productivity," *Social Forces* (March 1951), pp. 267–72.

17. D. Crane, "Scientists at Major and Minor Universities: A Study of

Productivity and Recognition," *American Sociological Review* (October 1965), pp. 699–714.

18. Jauch and Glueck, p. 68.

19. D. A. Katz, "Faculty Salaries, Promotions and Productivity at a Large University," *American Economic Review* (June 1973), pp. 469–77.

20. Ibid., p. 473.

21. H. P. Tuckman, J. H. Gapinski and R. P. Hagemann, "Faculty Skills and Salary Structure in Academe," *American Economic Review* (September 1977): pp. 692–702.

22. For example, two studies that use this method are: Jauch and Glueck, pp. 68–69; and Tuckman, Gapinski and Hagemann, pp. 694–95.

23. D. R. House and J. H. Yeager, "The Distribution of Publication Success within and among Top Economics Departments: A Disaggregated View of Recent Evidence," *Economic Inquiry* (October 1978), pp. 593–98; and J. G. Bell and J. J. Seater, "Publishing Performance: Departmental and Individual," *Economic Inquiry* (October 1978), pp. 599–615.

24. R. Smith and F. E. Fiedler, "The Measurement of Scholarly Work: A Critical Review of the Literature," *Educational Record* (Summer 1971), pp. 225–32.

25. G. J. Stigler and C. Friedland, "The Citation Practices of Doctorates in Economics," *Journal of Political Economy* (1975), pp. 477–507.

26. Smith and Fiedler, p. 228.

27. S. Cole and J. R. Cole, "Scientific Output and Recognition: A Study in the Operation of the Reward System in Science," *American Sociological Review* (June 1967), pp. 377–90.

28. Ibid.

29. A. M. Cartter, *An Assessment of Quality in Graduate Education* (Washington, D.C.: American Council on Education), 1966.

30. Smith and Fiedler, pp. 229–30.

31. Jauch and Glueck, pp. 66–75.

32. Smith and Fiedler, p. 230.

33. Jauch and Glueck, p. 67.

34. K. D. Roose and C.J. Anderson, *A Rating of Graduate Programs* (Washington, D.C.: American Council on Education), 1970.

35. D. Crane, "Scientists at Major and Minor Universities: A Study of Productivity and Recognition," *American Sociological Review* (October 1965), pp. 699–714.

36. Cole and Cole, p. 390.

Chapter 7

The Evaluation of Service and Citizenship

Many colleges and universities include service, along with teaching and research, when stating their missions. The role of service and the weight to be assigned to it in any evaluation process is often nebulous. Frequently, service is regarded as a catchall designed to reflect activities deemed of value, but which are not easily classified as either teaching or research. The questions to be considered then are whether service can be defined independently and, if so, how it can be measured.

While many studies in the academic literature have concentrated on the role and evaluation of research and teaching in university life, much less attention has been paid by researchers to the role of service or its evaluation. Although the lack of attention may be due to the inherent difficulties in defining service, another reason for the paucity of work in the area is the slight weight given to service at many universities and colleges. For example, Lin, McKeachie and Tucker surveyed twelve senior members of the Psychology Department at the University of Michigan.[1] Each member of the department was asked the percentage weighting that they assigned to teaching, research and service in promotion decisions. In this small sample, the sum of the mean weight assigned to teaching plus the mean weight assigned to research totaled over ninety-six percent. Only two of the twelve surveyed faculty assigned any positive weight at all to service. Other surveys of faculty confirm that faculty believe that service has little effect upon rewards received.[2]

While many faculty believe that service is an activity that is not rewarded, studies of faculty salary structure reveal otherwise. Administrative service as a dean or chairperson provides ample financial rewards.[3] Because administrative activities do not directly serve the primary mission of a university or college (i.e., education) and cannot be assessed in that light, evaluation of such service will be treated separately from other types of faculty service.

Hours spent on committee assignments and unpaid consulting are activities more commonly associated with faculty service. Several studies report small, but statistically significant rewards to one or both of these activities.[4] Thus, service activities receive some weight in salary determination despite their lack of importance in promotion and tenure decisions.

ETHICAL CONSIDERATIONS IN THE EVALUATION OF SERVICE

Given that some importance is attached to service, what ethical and behavioral considerations should enter into its evaluation? If service is to carry weight in determination of salary and if the incentive structure thereby created is to be consistent with the mission of the employing institution, then service by a faculty member must further the goals of the college or university that employs him or her. As well, to avoid misunderstandings, categories of activities that meet this criterion should be enumerated to the fullest extent possible. Such an enumeration, however, requires attention to several issues, the resolution of which (at least implicitly) reflects institutional ethical standards.

Many universities and colleges consider as meritorious only those service activities that require the use of professional expertise or experience. While they are frequently laudable, personal services are not readily associated with and do not advance the missions of the institution. For example, a faculty member's service to the community as a scout leader will not be materially associated with the university at which he or she is employed. Because, with few exceptions, only professional activities bring recognition to an academic institution and service its educational mission directly, only those activities should be customarily counted as service.

Occasionally, universities and colleges undertake tasks that, although not immediately related to any professional mission, are meant to increase the visibility of the institution in the local community. If faculty devote substantial time to the project, then their efforts are frequently construed as furthering the goals of the school. For example, if a university emphasizes its charitable contributions to the local community as a means of improving public relations, then service as chair of the drive might be counted as service because it advances that aim. The view taken here, however, is that this type of activity does not constitute service because it does not serve the *educational* mission of the institution. If such endeavors are to be rewarded, then they are properly rewarded as administrative activity, rather than professional service per se. Accordingly, remuneration of these activities cannot be assessed directly in terms of the primary mission of the institution.

Because only professional service is to be evaluated, one is then confronted with the issue of determining precisely which activities fall into this category. The difficulty is that many activities customarily classified as service could equally well be thought of as research or teaching. Refereeing articles for a professional journal is usually thought of as service. Just as easily, however, refereeing could be viewed as an adjunct to a professor's research program and categorized as research. A presentation delivered to a local community organization might be classified as either service or an extension of a faculty member's teaching. If service is to be evaluated objectively, then as precise a delineation as possible must be constructed so that members of a faculty can plan their service appropriately.

At almost all postsecondary educational institutions, appointment to a faculty position carries with it certain expectations of good citizenship. While attendance at departmental faculty meetings is an integral part of the self-governance responsibilities of a faculty member, the attendance is rarely rewarded. That is, a faculty appointment demands the performance of certain activities as a condition for the maintenance of the appointment. Thus, even though they are valuable, these activities should not be rewarded because they are required of all faculty as minimal behavioral standards to retain their positions. Again, to avoid confusion, faculty must be informed explicitly about the criteria used to differentiate service from expected good citizenship.

A more general problem that arises in the evaluation of service is to what degree activities of faculty that include elements of self-interested behavior constitute service. Obvious cases that must be addressed are whether paid consulting and teaching continuing education courses (for pay) constitute service. Because the faculty member is already remunerated directly by the hiring agent, many institutions do not reward the activity further through salary increments. McCarthy reports that in a survey of 156 public and private postsecondary institutions, approximately thirty percent explicitly state that they do not recognize as community service any activity for which remuneration is received.[5]

Even if no remuneration is received, a number of activities sometimes classified as service also contain elements of self-interested behavior. A professor who obtains a grant from outside sources benefits his employer because grants usually provide resources to the educational institution at which the professor is employed. At the same time, however, the grant benefits directly the professor who obtains it. Grantsmanship is a marketable skill that adds to the resume of the individual who obtains one. As well, grants frequently provide funds for a faculty member (if he or she desires) to buy back his time from his school in order to better pursue the funded program of research. Research grants, then, yield private benefits to the investigators and more general benefits to the university where they are employed. A second example of an activity in which self-interest enters, but for which there is no direct remuneration, is service on academic committees that are empowered to allocate presumably scarce resources. Faculty on such committees are seldom disinterested. Typically, they are members of competing groups within the institution. By representing their groups, committee members advance, not only the group interests, but their own as well. Where an activity contains aspects of both self-interest and public interest, the question remains whether the two can be separated and, hence, about the degree to which the activity should be counted as service in assessing salaries.

A BASIS FOR SERVICE EVALUATION

Difficulties in defining service and its role have sharply limited its importance at many universities and colleges. While there are many factors that circumscribe the role of service, the rest of the chapter is devoted to the development of a possible framework within which to define service activities consistently. The approach taken here equates service with the production of what economists call positive externalities (i.e., third-party effects). Specifically, service to a given unit is said to exist when an activity is performed that benefits that unit, but for which the individual performing the activity does not receive full compensation. Only insofar as the activity produces social benefit which exceeds the individual's (private) compensation should it count as service.

In a study of the history of several of the social sciences, Slaughter and Silva contend that service played a significant role in the emergence of those disciplines. They state:

Service allowed social scientists to act as "experts," bringing research skills to bear on pressing social problems. In this capacity, they were able to demonstrate the utility of their new social science and claim public and private resources for its support.[6]

To the extent to which a college or university directly benefits from the demonstration of the usefulness of the knowledge that is created and disseminated by its constituent disciplines, service advances the missions of the school. In this context, the acquisition by an educational institution of support, both political and financial, is the external benefit generated by service.

A word of caution is in order. While a faculty member may be commended for his efforts in service, the efforts alone cannot be rewarded. What must be demonstrated for remuneration is the actual gain to the department or school in excess of the individual's compensation. Thus, it is the beneficial effects of the activity that are valued, and not the activity per se. For example, unpaid consulting in the local community, if performed incompetently, may generate more antipathy than benefit for a school. Further, presumption of effect from the mere listing of activities creates perverse incentives in the performance of those tasks. It is all too common to observe faculty putting little effort into service activities because they receive credit for the activity by their mere presence, rather than for any results the activity may generate.

Another factor to weigh in measuring the external benefits of service endeavors is the degree to which the external benefits actually accrue to the institution where the provider is employed. Slaughter and Silva document only that a discipline as a whole prospers when service is undertaken by academicians.[7] At issue, however, is the degree to which individual institutions prosper as the discipline attracts resources. As there is an increase in available government and private grants in a subject area, major research universities can be expected to benefit disproportionately in competition for those grants, while regional universities and small colleges remain little affected. What must be demonstrated, then, is that not just a faculty member's field of study has gained from his service, but that the institution that employs him or her benefits. Ironically, the major research universities whose interests are most closely tied to the health of the disciplines represented by their constituent departments frequently place little explicit emphasis on service at all. They view such activities as merely good citizenship.

If service may be defined as the generation of a positive externality, and if the nature of the externality can be specified, one can measure the amount of service inherent in the activity. Assuming the externality exists, the degree to which a representative faculty member could be expected to undertake the activity allows one to ascertain the degree to which the activity elicits self-interested behavior. That activity deserves reward as service to the extent that it generates external benefits, but would not be undertaken by individual faculty, taking into account both good citizenship requirements and self-interested behavior. The appropriate additional reward, therefore, provides the additional incentive required to encourage further efforts in the activity. Of course, careful consideration must be given to both the costs and benefits in determining the optimal amount of service to be performed. The incentives should be adjusted to evoke that optimum.

In applying this measurement criterion, one must be careful to consider the willingness of a representative faculty member to provide the service, rather than determining whether any particular individual would undertake the service. Incorrectly applied on an individual basis, the criterion would penalize those faculty who were more public spirited and less self-interested. They would receive fewer rewards for the same service because they are more willing to do the work without recompense than are other faculty.

There is also the difficulty in defining the qualities of a representative member of the faculty. One could simply take the average characteristics of the faculty as representative. Such a procedure would be efficient in that it draws forth near optimal allocation of effort. There might be, however, normative objections to the incentives. For example, if all members of a faculty had no interest in governance of the unit, then should attendance at faculty meetings be rewarded as service? Sometimes the application of the criterion may yield unappealing incentives. The efficiency of the results must be balanced against prevailing normative standards of academic conduct in the construction of an appropriate set of incentives and sanctions.

What is clear from the literature on the evaluation of service is that at many institutions service is little regarded. Where it is regarded, it is poorly defined. Further, the rewards to be derived from demonstrated service are almost uniformly unclear. This chapter has attempted to present some of the questions that can and should be raised in the evaluation and reward of service. Obviously, there is no unique policy on the evaluation of service that will accommodate the missions of all units in all institutions. Given the missions of a unit, service should be evaluated in a manner consistent with the advancement of those missions. That is, care should be taken to ensure that the incentive system employed actually produces behavior from the faculty that is socially desirable. Finally, the policy for the evaluation of service must be as explicit and as objective as possible so that it is clearly understood. Only then can faculty adapt their behavior to the incentives created.

CITIZENSHIP

There is often a great deal of confusion concerning the differences between citizenship and service. Citizenship is what is expected of faculty members as their minimum contribution to the joint efforts of the academic unit so that it may continue to function. Citizenship, unlike service, does not necessarily require the application of substantial professional expertise or knowledge.

The differences between citizenship and service can and have been debated at length. For example, committee activities serve as a good point of departure when one tries to differentiate between citizenship and service. Promotion and tenure committee activities generally require the application of professional knowledge and expertise. To determine the fitness of a candidate for tenure requires some knowledge of teaching and research quality. Thus, committee activity of this sort contains elements of service. At the same time, these activities are necessary to the well-being of the academic unit and so contain important aspects of citizenship. Committee activities concerning curriculum, instructional development and self- governance may all require professional inputs in varying degrees. Service on a social committee, a traffic appeals committee or an athletic oversight committee requires little or no professional inputs. Accordingly, only citizenship is being rendered.

Service is professionally based; citizenship may include behavior in a broader scope than one's profession. Acting as a referee or editor is clearly service to one's profession; however, there may be elements of citizenship evidenced by leadership and integrity. Administrative duties are often included in the service category to the extent that they are professional activities requiring professional expertise. If the administrative activity is purely one of record keeping, letter writing, and public relations, then it readily falls into the category of citizenship rather than service.

Citizenship is demonstrated in several other ways than formally organized activities. A willingness to contribute to the academic unit's success in simple ways is the mark of a good citizen. Attendance at faculty meetings, assisting colleagues with their teaching and research activities and helping to establish a collegial environment all constitute good citizenship.

Too often, citizenship is most notable in its absence. Most academics have served with persons who are self-centered, unwilling to assist colleagues, arrogant or disruptive. The lack of careful consideration of the needs of the institution and of fellow colleagues can be every bit as damaging as the failure to meet classes or to do research. Evaluation systems rarely bring scholars to account for citizenship. If citizenship is to be fostered, then faculty members must be accountable for it. That good citizenship should be a major portion of a promotion, tenure or salary increment decision is not appropriate. Nonetheless, if a faculty member exhibits major deficiencies in citizenship (e.g., academic dishonesty), then tenure should be denied or other sanctions applied sufficient to remedy such deficiencies.

Citizenship and service are not easily differentiated. As a result, they are often classified and evaluated as the same activity. There is danger in this categorization. If citizenship and service are not differentiated, then faculty are not directly accountable for each. If enough faculty substitute one for the other, then the activity not undertaken may be lacking in aggregate. While it is often difficult to distinguish citizenship from service, it is incumbent upon the faculty and administration to make the effort if both are valued.

EVALUATION OF ADMINISTRATIVE SERVICE[8]

Academic administrators typically occupy positions of intermediate authority. They are usually appointed by the governing body of the university or some higher-level administrator to serve at the pleasure of the appointing body or individual. At the same time, however, the administrative appointee must also serve the needs of the academic unit over which (s)he is given some authority. Simply, the administrator serves as liaison between the faculty of a unit and higher-level administration. The administrator not only represents the governing board and higher-level administration to the faculty, but must represent the will of the faculty to higher-level administrators as well.

The dual nature of the administrator's duties dictates that the administrator be accountable to both the appointing agent or body and the faculty the administrator represents. Only the appointing administrator or governing board is capable of assessing how well a subordinate administrator carries out the decisions and dictums of the institution's central administration (i.e., how well she or he fits into the management "team" of the institution). By the same token, only the faculty can judge how well an administrator is representing their interests to external bodies and how well the administrator handles the day-to-day operations of the unit. Because the administrator's actions bear directly on the proper functioning of two distinct constituencies, both must be given voice in any evaluative process.

Other identifiable constituencies, to the extent that they are affected by the administrator's activities, should be consulted too.

While the president or chancellor of an institution should have some leeway in determining the type of manager that best fits the institution, the faculty usually bear most directly the brunt of an administrator's actions. The faculty, therefore, must be accorded at least equal, if not the primary, voice in any evaluation process. To do otherwise will deprive faculty of their legitimate rights and will invite low morale at best and open rebellion at worst. The standard here is an application of the principle of shared responsibility enunciated in the *Policies, Documents and Reports*, the AAUP Redbook (relevant portions of which are included in the appendix).[9]

The question of what standards to employ in the evaluation of an administrator's service now arises. Just as faculty should have standards by which they know they will be judged, so should academic administrators. As the needs of different institutions will vary, so will the standards for administrative performance. Nevertheless, there are certain general precepts to be observed in the evaluation.

First and foremost, an academic administrator is head of an academic unit within and over which he or she has certain governance responsibilities. The manner in which the administrator discharges those responsibilities can and should be a factor of primary importance in assessment of his/her performance. A number of criteria may be used to gauge the quality of leadership in an academic unit.

Academic ethics require the maintenance of standards and values in order to deliver instructional programs that are coherent and consistent. Where standards and values are not maintained, chaos results because there is no consistent vision guiding the academic programs. Consequently, each individual faculty member is left to pursue whatever objectives she or he deems fit. Because the objectives pursued by individual faculty are likely to diverge widely, programs as a whole are likely to lack coherence.

Although the faculty must delineate those standards and values, the administrator should facilitate their emergence. Once in place, those standards must be implemented by the administrator. Moreover, the administrative head of a unit, through feedback to and from the faculty, plays a crucial role in the maintenance and revision of the standards. Thus, the skill with which the head of a unit plays these roles is a crucial factor in the continued development and well-being of the unit.

A successful administrator will have sufficient standards and the necessary negotiating skills to build and maintain internal consensus about appropriate academic standards and values. Care must be taken by the administrator that any internal consensus reflects constraints imposed by the external environment. Demands placed on a unit by accrediting bodies or limitations placed on the unit by the institution's mission statement must be fully taken into account for the unit to progress. The administrator plays not only the role of a negotiator, but also the role of an informant to the faculty he/she serves. The acumen that the administrator displays in these roles during the day-to-day governance of the unit should be a primary criterion used in the assessment of his or her performance.

Academic administrators must often represent their constituency to external agents. Examples of such representation are:

1. An administrator of a unit represents the unit at professional meetings for recruitment of new faculty or other purposes.
2. A dean represents his unit to the campus as a whole in order to obtain a fair share of resources.
3. A chancellor or a dean deals with businesses, alumni groups or other outside agencies in order to procure money for the institution or unit.

The vigor with which an administrator undertakes these responsibilities and the success he/she meets in achieving the objectives of the activities form another basis for evaluating administrative service.

Finally, the charge given an administrator upon her or his appointment may contain other, specific objectives that she or he must achieve. These objectives might include the restructuring of a unit or the attainment of accreditation. The terms of the charge form another obvious basis for judging performance.

Whatever criteria are used, the standards employed should be made as explicit as possible so that the administrator will know the objectives and, also, the resources and means available to meet them. Just as faculty should be aware of the standards by which their services will be judged, the same courtesy is due to academic administrators.

SUMMARY AND CONCLUSIONS

The lack of attention paid to service in the academic literature reflects the slight weight that it receives in promotion, tenure and salary increment decisions at most academic institutions. Only administrative service has been shown to receive substantial rewards.

The activities that constitute faculty service are difficult to specify precisely. They may be different at different universities, and they may be different in different departments at the same university. Yet, these activities should more or less meet certain criteria: they should be professional in nature; they should constitute more than good citizenship and they should further the missions of the unit and generate social benefits to that unit in excess of any private compensation to the individual.

Administrative service is more complex to evaluate because an administrator serves both the appointing agent and the faculty. To be legitimate, the evaluation process must give voice to both constituencies. Criteria that might be used to evaluate administrative service include the proficiency with which the administrator conducts the day-to-day operations of the unit, the degree to which the administrator maintains appropriate academic standards and the skill with which the administrator represents the unit to external constituencies.

Both faculty and administrators are entitled to a written statement of the standards to be used in the evaluation of their service. Those standards should be made as explicit as possible, so that individuals will know how their services will be judged. That is the essence of ethical performance assessment.

NOTES

1. Y. Lin, W. J. McKeachie and D. G. Tucker, "The Use of Student Ratings in Promotion Decisions," *Journal of Higher Education* (September/October 1984), pp. 583–89.

2. See S. M. Dornbusch, "Perspectives from Sociology: Organization Evaluation of Faculty Performances," in *Academic Rewards in Higher Education*, edited by D. R. Lewis and W. E. Becker, Jr. (Cambridge, Mass.: Ballinger), 1979; and M. B. McCarthy, "Continuing Education Service as a Component of Faculty Evaluation," *Lifelong Learning: The Adult Years* (May 1980), pp. 8–11, 24–25.

3. For example, see D. A. Katz, "Faculty Salaries, Promotions, and Productivity at a Large University," *American Economic Review* (June 1973), pp. 469–77; J. J. Siegfried and K. J. White, "Teaching and Publishing as Determinants of Academic Salaries," *Journal of Economic Education* (Spring 1973), pp. 90–98; H. P. Tuckman, *Publication, Teaching and the Academic Reward Structure* (Lexington, Mass.: Lexington Books), 1976, Chapter 4; H. P. Tuckman, J. H. Gapinski and R. P. Hagemann, "Faculty Skills and Salary Structure in Academe," *American Economic Review* (September 1977), pp. 692–702; and H. P. Tuckman and R. P. Hagemann, "An Analysis of the Reward Structure in Two Disciplines," *Journal of Higher Education* (July/August 1976), pp. 447–64.

4. See K. L. Kasten, "Tenure and Merit Pay as Rewards for Research, Teaching and Service at a Research University," *Journal of Higher Education*

(July/August 1984), pp. 500–14; Katz, p. 471; Tuckman, pp. 55–60; Tuckman, Gapinski and Hagemann, pp. 695–99; and Tuckman and Hagemann, pp. 450–53.

5. McCarthy, p. 11.

6. S. Slaughter and E. T. Silva, "Service and the Dynamics of Developing Fields," *Journal of Higher Education* (1983), pp. 481–89.

7. Ibid., p. 482.

8. The following section applies to the evaluation of service of administrators whose primary function is the governance of an academic unit (e.g., department chair, dean, provost or chancellor). All of these administrators have as their constituents the faculty of an institution and typically hold faculty appointments, which brings the services of the administrators within the purview of this chapter. Other administrators such as a vice chancellor of financial affairs or a registrar have little direct contact with the faculty at large. Evaluation of these personnel is beyond the scope of the present inquiry.

9. *Policies, Documents and Reports*, American Association of University Professors, 1990. (See Appendix.)

Part III

External Influence on Appraisal

Chapter 8

The Law and Performance Appraisal

For years, the judiciary refrained from asserting jurisdiction over matters concerning academe. The theory was that professors were in a unique position, because of their education and professional duties, to qualify them to make decisions concerning virtually all academic matters. The courts also reasoned that if there was judicial intrusion into academic matters, society's best interests would not be served. The courts simply adopted the prevalent professorial view that academic freedom was the basis upon which academic decisions should be founded. The courts' unwillingness to substitute their judgment for professorial determinations in academic matters has come to be known as the doctrine of academic abstention. Recent years, however, have witnessed an increased willingness of the courts to intervene in academic matters.[1]

The erosion of the doctrine of academic abstention has been accelerating in virtually every aspect of academic life. Courts have asserted jurisdiction over areas that were once thought to be virtually unassailable because of their central role in a professor's academic freedom, including the assigning of grades, granting degrees and even admissions to university programs.[2] The courts have been particularly active in matters concerning academic personnel decisions, and in particular, tenure and renewal decisions.

The courts have also demonstrated a willingness to intervene in matters that allege discrimination on the basis of race, gender, age, religion, place of national origin and handicap. The nexus between Title VII of the Civil Rights Act of 1964, as amended, and faculty performance appraisal is also obvious.[3]

Further complicating the legal environment is the matter of labor relations law. Private colleges and universities are under the jurisdiction of the National Labor Relations Act, as amended.[4] Public colleges and universities are generally governed by the state labor relations statutes peculiar to that jurisdiction.[5] This characteristic of the scope of labor relations law results in private schools having a different legal environment from their public sector counterparts. Making matters even more complicated, each of the thirty-eight states that have enacted state labor relations statutes have some differences in the requirements of those statutes.[6]

The final important aspect of the law concerning performance appraisal is an organic difference in colleges and universities. State colleges and universities are public employers, in other words, agencies of the state government. Because state universities are state agencies, there are a multitude of constitutional issues that arise that are of no legal concern for private colleges and universities.[7]

The purpose of this chapter is to provide a brief introduction to the legal environment of faculty performance appraisal. A brief description of the scope of statutory and common law that applies to faculty performance appraisal will be offered. Specific attention will then be turned to anti-discrimination law because this is where the greatest constraints on university decision making, as it is applied to performance appraisal, is to be found. Finally, a brief discussion of law and ethics in the promulgation and implementation of performance appraisal systems will be offered.

SCOPE OF LAW CONCERNING
PERFORMANCE APPRAISAL

In general there are three categories of law; these are: (1) constitutional law, (2) statutory law and (3) common law. Constitutional law concerns the application of the U.S. Constitution (or state constitutions) to controversies. Statutory law is legislatively made law that is enacted by the Congress or state legislatures. Common law is judge-made law, typically concerned with contracts, torts or issues of equity (injunctions). Each of these bodies of law has been found by the courts to apply to certain aspects of academic performance appraisal.

Unfortunately, the increasing rates of litigation in society in general, and specifically in academe, have complicated many aspects of performance appraisal. The law concerning performance appraisal could easily fill several volumes the size of this book. The purpose of this book was to serve as an introductory guide to performance appraisal and not as a detailed examination of the law. As with most subjects as broad and as important to the conduct of an organization as performance appraisal, if specific technical questions arise concerning the application or current status of law, those questions are best asked of qualified legal counsel.

The role of legal counsel, however, is not to write the performance appraisal program for any organization. The performance appraisal system must be tailored to the substantive needs of the organization and the faculty members who serve it. The role of legal counsel must be confined to answering specific legal questions and review of performance appraisal systems, so as to permit a professional opinion concerning the appraisal system's compliance with law. Because of the complicating effects of law, too often substantive decisions, unrelated to legal compliance, may be left in the hands of attorneys. Attorneys are trained in the law, and may know nothing of the specifics of an academic organization. The role of the faculty and administration is to formulate the appraisal system and the role of the attorney is to provide legal advice. The two roles must never become confused.

THE CIVIL RIGHTS ACT OF 1964

Colleges and universities are covered under Title VII of the Civil Rights Act of 1964. The purpose of this legislation is to prevent and remedy discrimination in employment, wages or other conditions of employment based on race, sex, place of national origin, religion, creed, age or handicap. Title VII is enforced by an administrative law agency, the Equal Employment Opportunity Commission (EEOC). Policies that result in any protected minority being discriminated against are unlawful, as is intended discrimination.[8] The judiciary has readily intervened in any aspect of performance appraisal that results in a protected class of persons or an individual being disadvantaged. Performance appraisal systems, and the resultant reward and punishment systems that may be used to implement appraisals, must be in compliance with antidiscrimination statutes.

There are also several state and local governments in the United States that have enacted antidiscrimination statutes that bear directly on evaluation policies within state colleges and universities. Most of the state and local statutes provide for the prohibition and remedy of the types of discrimination proscribed by the federal statutes and add little, if any, protections beyond those contemplated by the Congress of the United States in enacting the federal law.

What does all of this mean? Very simply, it is unlawful to directly discriminate on the basis of any characteristic that is specifically enumerated, or associated with the enumerated characteristics, in matters involving employment. That is, to consider a person's place of national origin, race or sex in a manner adverse to the person being evaluated is not permitted and can be remedied by the EEOC or courts. The remedies include cease and desist orders and suits for damages. In addition, even if no individual or group of individuals directly discriminates against a protected minority, policies that have the same effect are also prohibited.

Discrimination is inherent in any evaluation policy. It is perfectly permissible to discriminate on the basis of realistic market considerations in determining salaries, on the basis of quantity and quality of professional accomplishments in granting promotions or tenure and on the basis of defensible merit in determining the quantity and quality of professional accomplishments. In fact, performance based appraisal systems are systems designed for discriminating between the performances of individuals, but not between the physical, racial or gender characteristics of individuals.

An academic institution begins to encroach upon prohibited discrimination once it moves away from quality and quantity criteria in measuring professional accomplishments and moves toward treating different classes of persons differently. For example, in a recent controversy a full professor, aged 62, found that he was paid $3000 less than any associate professor in his department. He complained to the dean who explained that, because he was at the end of his career and not likely to move, there was no compelling reason to give him a market adjustment. Further, the dean maintained that the available resources had to be used to retain the productive younger faculty. The problem is that "younger" meant more likely to seek employment elsewhere. The age of the older, full professor does not form a legitimate basis for a difference in treatment when salaries are determined. In this particular case, the full professor was more productive in research and was at least as good in the classroom as those associate professors in his field who were paid substantially more. The university attorney, unfortunately, had to explain to the dean that market efficiency is very often limited by public policy and it is always the latter the courts will sustain if tested.

The citizenship aspects of performance appraisal become very important in certain types of prohibited discrimination. One of the more difficult forms of discrimination to identify and effectively remedy is sexual harassment. In its overt forms, it is obvious and can be easily remedied. The classic example is the tenured faculty member making sexual advances to an untenured faculty member. The intent of the senior faculty member is not relevant. If the advances are not desired by the junior faculty member, that is sufficient grounds for a finding of discriminatory sexual harassment. The implicit threat to the junior member is that, if (s)he does not accept the advances, there will be adverse consequences because the senior faculty member votes on his or her tenure. Thus, the junior faculty member could not be assured of a fair hearing on the merits of his or her case.

There are more difficult forms of sexual harassment with which to deal. Jokes, touching, sexist language, and consideration of such gender-related matters as pregnancy (or the possibility thereof), child care responsibilities, gender-related medical problems or marital status all can result in a threatening, uncomfortable and discriminatory work environment. Ethically, consideration of gender cannot be permitted a place in the work environment. Legally, if harm comes to someone because of gender, then remedy can be sought through suits for damages and through cease and desist orders. Such conduct, if it occurs, is an appropriate consideration in performance appraisal and the citizenship dimension of performance appraisal provides at least one potential internal policy through which this form of discrimination can be remedied or prevented.

In formulating evaluation policies, the potential impact of those policies on specific protected groups must be recognized and accounted for where possible. This recognition is crucial because certain protected groups, such as those whose native language is not English, have been subjected to systematic discrimination at universities in the United States. This discrimination is carried out by using such evaluation techniques as student questionnaires as the sole criterion for assessing teaching quality. The questionnaires may contain biased information, reflecting student prejudices against these foreign-born faculty members rather than an objective assessment of their skills.

Affirmative Action

The recruiting of new faculty and the policies used to evaluate existing faculty are often inextricably linked. Most colleges and universities subscribe to an affirmative action plan that is developed for the purposes of assuring that there will be no prohibited discrimination in hiring practices and of attempting to attract qualified protected group members to the faculty of that institution. The rationale for affirmative action is that educational programs prosper when delivered by a diversity of faculty, with the attendant diverse outlooks. Without commenting on the merits of affirmative action programs, the authors wish to comment on the relation of affirmative action to faculty evaluation policies.

The purpose of affirmative action programs is to attract qualified persons who are members of protected classes. For an affirmative action program to be appropriate, the term "qualified" is key. An ethical dilemma results if members of protected classes are hired who are not qualified to hold the positions for which they were recruited. If the affirmative action program results in the under-qualified or the unqualified being hired, then the appraisal system will become burdened with the correction of the problems associated with inappropriate recruiting. In a sense, the recruiting practices of an academic institution are the first steps in faculty appraisal. The recruiting criteria must be firmly grounded in the expectations contained in the faculty evaluation policies. It is discriminatory to hire from a protected class when available evidence on his or her professional qualifications demonstrates that the faculty member hired will be placed at a substantial disadvantage (based on proper evaluation criteria) in obtaining promotion, tenure or salary increments.

Other Antidiscrimination Statutes

There are numerous other federal statutes that are concerned with discrimination issues. Among these statutes are the Equal Pay Act of 1963, which prohibits wage discrimination against protected classes of employees,[9] and the Age Discrimination in Employment Act, which prohibits discrimination in employment or in the terms and conditions of employment on the basis of age.[10] These statutes are amendments or supplements to Title VII of the Civil Rights Act of 1964. They broaden the definitions of protected classes of employees so as to prohibit and remedy discrimination against persons based on individually uncontrollable, nonmerit factors.

The legal complications under the antidiscrimination law are many and varied. A detailed analysis of each aspect of the civil rights laws is beyond the scope of the present work. Fortunately, there are several excellent reviews of the current status of the antidiscrimination law in the United States. The reader is referred to these.[11] All that the authors have done here is to present a brief sketch of the salient features of this body of law for academic appraisal.

LAW AND ETHICS

Most Americans have become accustomed to the idea that the courts play a significant and important role in determining how we will conduct our day-to-day business. There is, however, a very important reason why the observed importance of law has emerged. American society, as well as most industrialized societies, has become increasingly complex. As complexity increases, there is increased need for social control of individual activities to assure that chaos does not replace order.

As discussed in Part I, ethical and moral standards of conduct are almost always important issues of social control and remain so even in the face of the development of law. Law develops as a result of the need to be able to enforce standards of conduct and to fill gaps between the commonly accepted morals and ethics of a society. History teaches that ethics and law are intimately related.

In the context of faculty appraisal, ethics and law are often substitutes for one another. That is, if the ethics of a college or other academic unit are either deficient or missing, the recourse left to faculty members to ensure fair and ethical treatment is litigation. Ethical standards cannot ensure that there will not be litigation of appraisal issues. Individuals may still find it in their self-interest to sue, even in the presence of a strong ethical base. A strong ethical basis for relations among faculty may be the best insurance against litigation and adverse judgments in court. If appraisals and personnel decisions are founded in proper ethical bases that are in compliance with legal standards, then litigation is rarely a significant problem.

Public opinion within an academic institution is often a function of the collective academic standards and morals of the individual faculty members and of the leadership provided by administrative officers and senior faculty members. Public opinion is almost always important, not only in determining the policies that will govern an academic institution, but also in shaping and forming the ethical base of the school. In some respects, ethics, while more enduring, are indeed tied to public opinion. In turn, public opinion often forms the basis for legislative action both in the governance of a college or university and in the formulation of public policy.

Law, ethics, morals and public opinion are all highly interrelated and cannot be totally separated, except for the purpose of academic discourse. The effects of these social control mechanisms, however, are substantially different. Litigation produces judgments that are externally enforceable. Ethics, on the other hand, produce judgments, often informal, that are enforceable only if the institution makes internal provisions for their enforcement. Codification and enforcement mechanisms for ethical conduct are not uncommon in the professions, and they exist in almost all academic institutions as well. Public opinion, however, contains no element of formal control except to the extent that it forms the basis for ethical codification or law. The informal control that can be exerted through public opinion amounts to little more than a source of conflict and beginning focal point for more substantive action.

IMPACT OF LAW

The legal environment has complicated the creation and implementation of evaluation policies. The statutory requirements imposed by the external legal environment should be taken as the minimum ethical standards for personnel evaluation. In other words, if a university's policies run afoul of the law there are often serious ethical deficiencies. There is no doubt that personnel matters, including evaluation, have become more complex and likely to require litigation. Consequently, those charged with the responsibility for the formulation and implementation of such policies need to be more aware of ethical considerations and legal requirements. It may also mean that rules and policies need to be more specific and clearer than in past years.

Many fear that the United States is a nation that has become far too litigation prone. Such charges may or may not be valid. The simple fact remains that there is much to be gained by being aware of faculty rights and obligations. To be ethical requires operating in such a manner as to ensure that those rights and obligations are properly promulgated and strictly observed.

SUMMARY AND CONCLUSIONS

The legal environment is a complex and extensive constraint on personnel policies, including evaluation. In general, public and private university employers are subject to a wide and varied body of statutory, constitutional and common law. Legal advice may often be necessary to ensure that the formulation and implementation of appraisal systems is in compliance with law. That does not mean lawyers should write faculty performance appraisal systems; in fact, the attorney's role should be limited to providing legal guidance.

Antidiscrimination law was among the first bodies of statutory law to encroach upon the doctrine of academic abstention. The review of anti-discrimination law demonstrates that performance based appraisal systems must, in fact, be based on defensible performance based criteria. If criteria that are not performance based are used to appraise faculty members, the institution creates a potential for litigation.

Each particular body of law is designed to protect certain employee rights that have been deemed to be in the public interest. Faculty members and academic administrators must be aware that there is a substantial collection of law that governs personnel actions. Rather than attempting simply to meet minimum legal requirements, academic units should formulate their evaluation policies firmly based upon ethical standards. By establishing ethical standards, legal standards may never become an issue.

NOTES

1. Terrance Leas, "Higher Education, the Courts and the 'Doctrine' of Academic Abstention," *Journal of Law and Education*, vol. 20, no. 2 (Spring 1991), pp. 135–65.

2. Robert L. Cherry and John P. Geary, "The College Catalog as a Contract," *Journal of Law and Education*, vol. 21, no. 1 (Winter 1992), pp. 1–32.

3. 78 Stat. 241, 253–266 (1964) as amended by 86 Stat. 103 (1972), and 88 Stat. 192 (1975).

4. 49 Stat. 449 (1935), as amended by 61 Stat. 136 (1947), 65 Stat. 601 (1951), 72 Stat. 945 (1958), 73 Stat. 541 (1959), and 88 Stat. 395 (1974).

5. David A. Dilts, Clarence R. Deitsch and Ali Rassuli, *Labor Relations Law in State and Local Government* (Westport, Conn.: Quorum Books), 1992.

6. Ibid.

7. *Pickering v. Board of Education*, 391 U.S. 563 (1968) is the landmark case in the matter of state governments and their subdivisions having the specific limitations of the rights guaranteed people by the 14th Amendment to the U.S. Constitution.

8. *Griggs v. Dukes Power Company*, 401 U.S. 424 (1971).

9. This statute appears as Section 6(d) of the Fair Labor Standards Act, 52 Stat. 1060, as amended.

10. 29 U.S.C. para. 621 et seq.

11. William Murphy, Julius Getman and James Jones, *Discrimination in Employment*, 4th ed. (Washington, D.C.: Bureau of National Affairs, Inc.), 1979.

Chapter 9

Collective Bargaining
and Faculty Evaluation

The purpose of this chapter is to introduce unions in academe and the concept of collective bargaining as it affects academic performance appraisal. A brief discussion of administration under union contracts and its impact on performance will also be offered.

Collective bargaining can be conceptualized as three not altogether distinct activities. These three activities are union organizing, contract negotiations and contract administration. The overlap of these activities is often substantial, thus, their division into general categories is somewhat artificial, but useful for present purposes. Organizational activities concern the formation and certification of a labor organization as exclusive representative of the employees, and the establishment of a bargaining relationship between that organization and the management. Contract negotiations concern the creation of an agreement outlining the respective rights of the parties. Contract administration is the exercise and enforcement of those rights.

Keeping in mind that these activities overlap, one may now examine collective bargaining in colleges and universities. The discussion here focuses upon the negotiation and administration of evaluation policies, even though those processes represent only a narrow portion of the issues subject to collective bargaining in most jurisdictions.

COLLECTIVE BARGAINING DEFINED

Collective bargaining is a system of labor-management relations under which labor and management mutually determine the terms and conditions of employment.[1] Mutual determination requires that the representatives of employees (not the employees themselves) and the representatives of the employer (not the taxpayers or governing body themselves) meet and confer for the purpose of setting the terms and conditions of employment.

The terms and conditions of employment are one common definition of "scope" of bargaining. The scope of bargaining may be thought of as that collection of issues that are the legal subjects of negotiations. The use of the language "terms and conditions of employment" is taken from the National Labor Relations Act, and some state and local jurisdictions have adopted this definition of the scope of bargaining in their statutes.[2] Other jurisdictions, however, provide "laundry lists" of issues that are subject to negotiations. These lists may or may not include the terms and conditions of employment. Some issues that are not terms and conditions of employment may be added to the list of negotiable items, while many issues that are terms and conditions of employment may be excluded from bargaining. (The exclusions are the most common.)

Under the federal law and virtually all of the state collective bargaining laws the procedures for performance appraisal are subject to collective bargaining. Only a very few state bargaining laws reserve the criteria of a performance appraisal system to management determination. In all cases, appeals and grievance procedures and the effects of the performance appraisal on salaries, tenure and promotion are also subject to collective bargaining.

UNION ORGANIZING

Although the percentage of unionized workers in the U.S. economy has declined over the past fifteen years, unionization in the public sector, particularly in education, has increased significantly over the period.

There has been little research concerning why professors join and form labor unions. What research has been conducted suggests that white collar employees in general, and college professors in particular, join unions for the same reasons as blue collar workers. That is, when employees believe that they no longer have an effective voice in determining the terms and conditions of employment, they often seek a mechanism by which such influence can be exerted. Wages, job security and organizational justice are also important determinants, but the single greatest factor appears to be "voice." Thus, it is surprising that university professors would be forming and joining unions because the tenets of academic freedom and the notions of shared responsibility would seem to provide the voice that professors value.

When faculty senates fail to influence the directions their institutions take and when shared responsibility becomes little more than a right to know what the administration has decided, then unionization has been the viable alternative selected by many faculty members to regain voice. Through the collective bargaining process, faculty voice becomes institutionalized and contractually protected. In faculty senate systems where no union exists, there may be no protections of voice that can be reasonably exerted. Again, just like in the blue collar world, professorial organizing is often the result of failed administration and sometimes the abrogation of the basic tenets of shared responsibility and academic freedom.

EVALUATION AND COLLECTIVE BARGAINING

Private colleges and universities are covered under the National Labor Relations Act, and evaluation criteria and procedures are mandatory issues of collective bargaining for all of these institutions. For those institutions covered by state statutes there are differences. Under some statutes (e.g., Kansas) the evaluative criteria are established by statute and are, therefore, not subject to negotiations. The procedures, however, are a mandatory issue of collective bargaining. Recognizing these differences and understanding the scope of bargaining under the statute that applies to the specific institution are important in determining what can and what cannot be negotiated.

The negotiation of criteria or procedures for evaluation of faculty performance is almost always a critical element of any collective bargaining agreement in higher education. Administrators will frequently view the evaluation process as an important element of managerial control. They will jealously guard what they perceive as legitimate administrative discretion. Conversely, faculty members and unions normally view evaluation issues as the core of job security and academic freedom. They will fight long and hard to ensure that the faculty maintains control over the process and the criteria. Thus, evaluative issues are almost always distributive bargaining issues, frequently among the most important and controversial of those issues.

The negotiation of evaluation criteria and procedures is but the first step in the process. (See the Appendix for AAUP statements on both evaluation and collective bargaining.) The parties to collective bargaining agreements have fashioned numerous solutions to the problems of what the criteria and procedures should be. Some differ very little from what would be expected in a collegial, self-governing academic institution, while others take on an aura of formality more often associated with federal employment.

There are those that give seniority a prominent role much the same as blue collar labor agreements. In short, there is little that can be offered in the way of generalization about the nature of evaluation provisions in collective bargaining agreements. The administration of evaluation processes may differ substantially when the process is negotiated as part of a collective bargaining agreement. Under a collective bargaining agreement, evaluations are typically issues that can be taken to a grievance procedure that ends with final and binding arbitration by a neutral third party. In the absence of union representation, faculty infrequently have access to binding arbitration.

ADMINISTRATION OF THE
NEGOTIATION EVALUATION PROCESS

Among colleges and universities there are wide variations in how productivity data are gathered and weighed, in who is responsible for gathering evidence and in who is responsible for decision making. Further, there are frequently considerable differences concerning reviews of personnel decisions and the appeals procedures to be followed if a faculty member is dissatisfied. Often, in the absence of collective bargaining, the data-gathering and decision-making authority will be specifically delineated. In some instances, however, there may be important elements of the process that have not been reduced to writing. It is not uncommon for universities to make general statements about teaching, research, service and citizenship, but then fail to specify what types of evidence of merit in these areas are credible or valid. Under a collective bargaining regime, these issues are frequently raised and resolved because of the competitive nature of a bargaining relationship. When these issues are raised and specifically addressed in writing, then all parties know what to expect and there are fewer ambiguities to be resolved in administration. When ambiguities do arise, the collective bargaining agreement almost always specifies a grievance procedure, with time limits for raising and answering grievances. In addition, the agreement identifies the authorities responsible for dealing with the problems.

It is not necessary that a collective bargaining agreement exist to ensure procedural due process and institutional justice. In fact, union-like grievance procedures have been adopted in both the private and public sector in the absence of collective bargaining. What is certain is that where a formal appeals process does not exist or fails to specify time limits for action, there is no method to ensure that a grievance will be processed; thus procedural due process is denied and the perception of institutional justice significantly eroded.

The formalized grievance procedure that results in a final and binding award by a disinterested third party ensures an element of institutionalized fairness that does not exist otherwise. Under most nonunion processes, there is no determination of whether a faculty member was treated fairly or properly by a disinterested neutral unless that faculty member is willing and financially able to sue. In response, many universities have opted for an ombudsman system that can end in the ombudsman's acting as arbitrator to provide the institutionalized fairness which cannot be provided through peer or administrative review. Both peer and administrative review suffer from a lack of specific and enforceable ethics that bind a professional arbitrator to neutrality and to conduct proceedings in a consistent manner, giving each party an equal opportunity to be heard. This alone is why many major universities (e.g., California at Berkeley—David Feller, Michigan State—Jack Stieber, and the University of Iowa—Tony Sinicropi) have chosen professional labor arbitrators as their ombudsmen.

Peer and administrative review is conducted within the institution by parties who are neither trained nor experienced neutrals. Often, they have specific individual loyalties and may be subject to political caprice. Peer or administrative review of appeals may provide some elements of procedural due process. They may even result in fair decisions, but there are no checks and balances. On the other hand, experienced neutrals bound by a code of professional ethics guarantee such results.

Perhaps more than anything else, collective bargaining provides for the grievance/arbitration process that, in turn, ensures institutional due process and fairness, which are simply not available without the arms-length negotiation of a grievance procedure that ends in arbitration.[3]

SUMMARY AND CONCLUSIONS

There are several elements which comprise collective bargaining; the organization of labor, plus the negotiation and administration of a collective bargaining agreement, were examined in this chapter. The organization of college professors is not unique. College professors appear to join and form unions for the same reasons as other professionals and blue collar workers. The single greatest motivation for joining and forming unions is to gain voice in decisions concerning those issues that are most important to the employees. These issues include the criteria and procedures affecting wages, job security and relative rights.

Contract negotiations are often examined from the naive view that one conceptual model can explain the complex process of bargaining. The process of bargaining is a system of economic and behavioral activities.

Evaluation procedures and criteria are mandatory issues of collective bargaining under most labor-relations acts. There is little evidence that suggests that the processes and criteria are either the same or different under collective bargaining than in its absence. What is different is that collective bargaining agreements specify grievance procedures that result, by design, in procedural due process and institutional justice. The peer and administrative review processes of nonunion institutions cannot provide, except by chance, the same levels of due process or fairness. Formal grievance procedures, however, can be used in the absence of collective bargaining. With either an ombudsman or arbitrator, they can provide the same results as are traditionally observed in collective bargaining grievance procedures.

NOTES

1. David A. Dilts and Clarence R. Deitsch, *Labor Relations* (New York: Macmillan Publishing Company), 1983, pp. 5–7.

2. Section 8(d) 61 Stat. 136 as amended by 73 Stat. 519, commonly called the Taft-Hartley Act.

3. See Dilts and Deitsch, Chapter 9.

Chapter 10

Epilogue: Rewards and Results

The purpose of this chapter is twofold. First, it will connect the appraisal system with the universities' reward and punishment systems. Appraisal is but one dimension of effective university administration and self-governance. Without appropriate connections between the performance appraisal system and the reward and punishment structure, appraisal becomes a meaningless exercise at the individual level. The appraisal system could still provide useful information for monitoring total organizational performance, but the incentive effects of individual assessments to improve organizational performance would be lost.

There are several conclusions that must be drawn from the work presented in this text. The final mission of this chapter is to present these general conclusions.

MAKING APPRAISAL MEANINGFUL

Performance appraisal is, at best, a meaningless exercise at the individual level, unless it forms the basis for predictable and fair personnel decisions that motivate individuals to cooperate in the accomplishment of the organization's academic goals. In other words, performance appraisal is the basis upon which promotion, tenure, renewal and salary decisions are made. It is not enough to create a fair and ethical performance appraisal system without identifying how the measured performance will be translated into rewards and punishments.

Researchers have found that the failure to adequately link performance assessment with compensation has several negative implications.[1] Rewards that have been legitimately earned and withheld have been found to be one of the most punishing of all possible outcomes.[2] It has also been shown that a lack of predictability of rewards serves to mitigate commitment and increase employee dissatisfaction.[3] In other words, for performance appraisal to provide a basis for extrinsic motivation it must result in predictable rewards for professional accomplishments. If the appraisal system fails in either predictability or in the requisite nexus between performance and rewards, it has the potential for providing disincentives to quality performance.

The performance appraisal system must also provide fair warning of what is expected. If the levels of productivity specified in the appraisal policy are attained and promotion or tenure are not granted, then litigation and poor faculty morale are likely outcomes. Salaries are also serious matters. The salary structure within specific fields will need to reflect external labor market requirements, but within the specific institution salaries must reflect the relative productivity of faculty members.

The external labor market will almost always prove to be a constraint on a pure merit system. For example, professors in engineering, business, medicine and law have historically been paid more than faculty members in education, arts and sciences and home economics. This observation is the result of the forces of supply and demand in the market. Whether the market produces fair results is subject to debate; the fact is that if a college or university is to attract and retain appropriately qualified faculty members the prevailing market wage will have to be paid.

Once professors have joined a faculty the matter of internal salary structure becomes very important. Within specific academic disciplines there may still be some market differences. For example, in business administration, finance professors are typically more scarce than economists and therefore command a higher salary. Within finance or economics, however, there should be a distribution of salaries that reflect the relative worth of the respective faculty members' professional accomplishments. In other words, the performance appraisal system must be sufficiently accurate and reliable so as to permit salary differentials based upon the relative productivity of faculty members.[4]

High turnover rates, a lack of commitment, low productivity, increased political turmoil and increased professorial dissatisfaction are common symptoms of failed performance systems.[5] To prevent the numerous difficulties associated with inappropriate appraisal and rewards, the appraisal system must be effective in determining who has done what, and in rewarding or punishing that productivity accordingly.

Politics and Performance Appraisal

Without a specific and predictable evaluation and reward system, politics may become the basis for decisions. In such systems, ethics and efficiency may still be served, but not because of a system designed to ensure ethical and efficient personnel decisions. The central benefit of having a written appraisal process is that it ensures continuity of policy and potentially systematic appraisal over time. The written page is far better at reflecting what the organization intends than some nebulous institutional memory.

Standards are necessary, and accountability in the administration of those standards is also necessary. Neither standards nor accountability alone is sufficient to assure quality faculty performance; both are needed.

Ethics and Rewards

Ethics and economic rationality need not be strangers. As central as ethics are to appraisal systems, the economic incentives and behaviors they are designed to elicit must conform to the same high ethical standards expected of the appraisal system. The nexus established between performance levels and rewards should reflect the relative value of the contributions to the organization's mission of those performance characteristics. At the same time, those levels of performance should also reflect the overall value of the contributions generally held in academe.

Over the past few decades excellence in teaching has been relatively ignored in reward systems. There is no ethical compulsion to reward average teaching beyond what is currently observed, but if the recent change in academic values toward a higher priority for excellence in teaching is an ethical and legitimate change in directions, we should expect to observe greater rewards for faculty members who have attained a level of instructional effectiveness that can be shown to be excellent. To give lip service to excellence in teaching and fail to reward faculty efforts in attaining that level of performance is substantially lacking in ethics.

CONCLUSIONS

The purpose of this book was to present what is known of the evaluation of teaching, research, citizenship and service. Performance appraisal does not occur in a vacuum and the legal environment as well as collective bargaining are binding constraints on the freedom to construct and administer appraisal systems. Ethics in the formulation and administration of performance appraisal systems were also integrated into the discussions offered. If appraisal systems are to serve organizations and faculty members they must be based on sound academic ethics.

The evaluation of research and teaching has been subjected to considerable analysis and much is known about both subjects. Service and citizenship in academe have not been as well researched; however, what useful conclusions have been drawn concerning these subjects have been presented.

There is no secret formula for the construction and implementation of ethical performance appraisal systems. The academic research provides a basis for establishing appropriate criteria for appraisal, but the selection of those criteria and structure of assessment procedures must be tailored to the specific needs of the faculty and the organization they serve, if it is to be effective. The mission and culture of the specific college or university will do much to determine what is expected of the performance appraisal system.

It is hoped that this book will aid the novice evaluator, faculty members and policymakers in their quest for ethical performance appraisal systems that assist in the attainment of excellence in higher education.

NOTES

1. R. M. Madigan and D. J. Hoover, "Effects of Alternative Job Evaluation Methods on Decisions Involving Pay Equity," *Academy of Management Journal*, vol. 29 (1986), pp. 84–100.

2. J. Greenberg, "Determinants of Perceived Fairness of Performance Evaluations," *Journal of Applied Psychology*, vol. 71 (1986), pp. 340–52.

3. G. Meng, "Link Pay to Job Evaluation," *Personnel Journal* (March 1990), pp. 98–104.

4. Donald P. Schwab and L. Dyer, "Motivational Impact of a Compensation System on Employee Performance," *Organizational Behavior and Human Performance*, vol. 9 (1973), pp. 215–25.

5. Edward Lawler, *Pay and Organizational Effectiveness* (New York: McGraw-Hill), 1971.

Appendix

Selected Excerpts from
AAUP Policy Documents
and Reports

1940 Statement of Principles on Academic Freedom and Tenure

With 1970 Interpretive Comments

In 1940, following a series of joint conferences begun in 1934, representatives of the American Association of University Professors and of the Association of American Colleges agreed upon a restatement of principles set forth in the 1925 Conference Statement on Academic Freedom and Tenure. *This restatement is known to the profession as the 1940* Statement of Principles on Academic Freedom and Tenure.

The 1940 Statement *is printed below, followed by Interpretive Comments as developed by representatives of the American Association of University Professors and the Association of American Colleges during 1969. The governing bodies of the associations, meeting respectively in November 1989 and January 1990, adopted several changes in language in order to remove gender-specific references from the original text.*

The purpose of this statement is to promote public understanding and support of academic freedom and tenure and agreement upon procedures to assure them in colleges and universities. Institutions of higher education are conducted for the common good and not to further the interest of either the individual teacher[1] or the institution as a whole. The common good depends upon the free search for truth and its free exposition.

Academic freedom is essential to these purposes and applies to both teaching and research. Freedom in research is fundamental to the advancement of truth. Academic freedom in its teaching aspect is fundamental for the protection of the rights of the teacher in teaching and of the student to freedom in learning. It carries with it duties correlative with rights.[1][2]

Tenure is a means to certain ends; specifically: (1) freedom of teaching and research and of extramural activities, and (2) a sufficient degree of economic security to make the profession attractive to men and women of ability. Freedom and economic security, hence, tenure, are indispensable to the success of an institution in fulfilling its obligations to its students and to society.

ACADEMIC FREEDOM

(a) Teachers are entitled to full freedom in research and in the publication of the results, subject to the adequate performance of their other academic duties; but research for pecuniary return should be based upon an understanding with the authorities of the institution.

(b) Teachers are entitled to freedom in the classroom in discussing their subject, but they should be careful not to introduce into their teaching controversial matter which has no relation to their subject.[2] Limitations of academic freedom because of religious or other aims of the institution should be clearly stated in writing at the time of the appointment.[3]

---

[1]The word "teacher" as used in this document is understood to include the investigator who is attached to an academic institution without teaching duties.

[2]Bold-face numbers in brackets refer to Interpretive Comments which follow.

(c) College and university teachers are citizens, members of a learned profession, and officers of an educational institution. When they speak or write as citizens, they should be free from institutional censorship or discipline, but their special position in the community imposes special obligations. As scholars and educational officers, they should remember that the public may judge their profession and their institution by their utterances. Hence they should at all times be accurate, should exercise appropriate restraint, should show respect for the opinions of others, and should make every effort to indicate that they are not speaking for the institution.[4]

ACADEMIC TENURE

After the expiration of a probationary period, teachers or investigators should have permanent or continuous tenure, and their service should be terminated only for adequate cause, except in the case of retirement for age, or under extraordinary circumstances because of financial exigencies.

In the interpretation of this principle it is understood that the following represents acceptable academic practice:

1. The precise terms and conditions of every appointment should be stated in writing and be in the possession of both institution and teacher before the appointment is consummated.
2. Beginning with appointment to the rank of full-time instructor or a higher rank,[5] the probationary period should not exceed seven years, including within this period full-time service in all institutions of higher education; but subject to the proviso that when, after a term of probationary service of more than three years in one or more institutions, a teacher is called to another institution it may be agreed in writing that the new appointment is for a probationary period of not more than four years, even though thereby the person's total probationary period in the academic profession is extended beyond the normal maximum of seven years.[6] Notice should be given at least one year prior to the expiration of the probationary period if the teacher is not to be continued in service after the expiration of that period.[7]
3. During the probationary period a teacher should have the academic freedom that all other members of the faculty have.[8]
4. Termination for cause of a continuous appointment, or the dismissal for cause of a teacher previous to the expiration of a term appointment, should, if possible, be considered by both a faculty committee and the governing board of the institution. In all cases where the facts are in dispute, the accused teacher should be informed before the hearing in writing of the charges and should have the opportunity to be heard in his or her own defense by all bodies that pass judgment upon the case. The teacher should be permitted to be accompanied by an advisor of his or her own choosing who may act as counsel. There should be a full stenographic record of the hearing available to the parties concerned. In the hearing of charges of incompetence the testimony should include that of teachers and other scholars, either from the teacher's own or from other institutions. Teachers on continuous appointment who are dismissed for reasons not involving moral turpitude should receive their salaries for at least a year from the date of notification of dismissal whether or not they are continued in their duties at the institution.[9]
5. Termination of a continuous appointment because of financial exigency should be demonstrably *bona fide*.

1940 INTERPRETATIONS

At the conference of representatives of the American Association of University Professors and of the Association of American Colleges on November 7–8, 1940, the following interpretations of the 1940 *Statement of Principles on Academic Freedom and Tenure* were agreed upon:

1. That its operation should not be retroactive.

2. That all tenure claims of teachers appointed prior to the endorsement should be determined in accordance with the principles set forth in the 1925 Conference Statement on Academic Freedom and Tenure.

3. If the administration of a college or university feels that a teacher has not observed the admonitions of paragraph (c) of the section on Academic Freedom and believes that the extramural utterances of the teacher have been such as to raise grave doubts concerning the teacher's fitness for his or her position, it may proceed to file charges under paragraph (a)(4) of the section on Academic Tenure. In pressing such charges the administration should remember that teachers are citizens and should be accorded the freedom of citizens. In such cases the administration must assume full responsibility, and the American Association of University Professors and the Association of American Colleges are free to make an investigation.

1970 INTERPRETIVE COMMENTS

Following extensive discussions on the 1940 Statement of Principles on Academic Freedom and Tenure *with leading educational associations and with individual faculty members and administrators, a joint committee of the AAUP and the Association of American Colleges met during 1969 to reevaluate this key policy statement. On the basis of the comments received, and the discussions that ensued, the joint committee felt the preferable approach was to formulate interpretations of the* Statement *in terms of the experience gained in implementing and applying the* Statement *for over thirty years and of adapting it to current needs.*

The committee submitted to the two associations for their consideration the following "Interpretive Comments." These interpretations were adopted by the Council of the American Association of University Professors in April 1970 and endorsed by the Fifty-sixth Annual Meeting as Association policy.

In the thirty years since their promulgation, the principles of the 1940 *Statement of Principles on Academic Freedom and Tenure* have undergone a substantial amount of refinement. This has evolved through a variety of processes, including customary acceptance, understandings mutually arrived at between institutions and professors or their representatives, investigations and reports by the American Association of University Professors, and formulations of statements by that association either alone or in conjunction with the Association of American Colleges. These comments represent the attempt of the two associations, as the original sponsors of the 1940 *Statement*, to formulate the most important of these refinements. Their incorporation here as Interpretive Comments is based upon the premise that the 1940 *Statement* is not a static code but a fundamental document designed to set a framework of norms to guide adaptations to changing times and circumstances.

Also, there have been relevant developments in the law itself reflecting a growing insistence by the courts on due process within the academic community which parallels the essential concepts of the 1940 *Statement*; particularly relevant is the identification by the Supreme Court of academic freedom as a right protected by the First Amendment. As the Supreme Court said in *Keyishian v. Board of Regents* 385 U.S. 589 (1967), "Our Nation is deeply committed to safeguarding academic freedom, which is of transcendent value to all of us and not merely to the teachers concerned. That freedom is therefore a special concern of the First Amendment, which does not tolerate laws that cast a pall of orthodoxy over the classroom."

The numbers refer to the designated portion of the 1940 *Statement* on which interpretive comment is made.

1. The Association of American Colleges and the American Association of University Professors have long recognized that membership in the academic profession carries with it special responsibilities. Both associations either separately or jointly have consistently affirmed these responsibilities in major policy statements, providing guidance to professors in their utterances as citizens, in the exercise of their responsibilities to the institution and to students, and in their conduct when resigning from their institution or when undertaking government-sponsored research. Of particular relevance is the *Statement on Professional Ethics*, adopted in 1966 as Association

policy. (A revision, adopted in 1987, was published in *Academe: Bulletin of the AAUP* 73 [July–August 1987]: 49.)

2. The intent of this statement is not to discourage what is "controversial." Controversy is at the heart of the free academic inquiry which the entire statement is designed to foster. The passage serves to underscore the need for teachers to avoid persistently intruding material which has no relation to their subject.

3. Most church-related institutions no longer need or desire the departure from the principle of academic freedom implied in the 1940 *Statement*, and we do not now endorse such a departure.

4. This paragraph is the subject of an Interpretation adopted by the sponsors of the 1940 *Statement* immediately following its endorsement which reads as follows:

> If the administration of a college or university feels that a teacher has not observed the admonitions of paragraph (c) of the section on Academic Freedom and believes that the extramural utterances of the teacher have been such as to raise grave doubts concerning the teacher's fitness for his or her position, it may proceed to file charges under paragraph (a)(4) of the section on Academic Tenure. In pressing such charges the administration should remember that teachers are citizens and should be accorded the freedom of citizens. In such cases the administration must assume full responsibility, and the American Association of University Professors and the Association of American Colleges are free to make an investigation.

Paragraph (c) of the 1940 *Statement* should also be interpreted in keeping with the 1964 "Committee A Statement on Extramural Utterances" (*AAUP Bulletin* 51 [1965]: 29), which states *inter alia*: "The controlling principle is that a faculty member's expression of opinion as a citizen cannot constitute grounds for dismissal unless it clearly demonstrates the faculty member's unfitness for his or her position. Extramural utterances rarely bear upon the faculty member's fitness for the position. Moreover, a final decision should take into account the faculty member's entire record as a teacher and scholar."

Paragraph V of the *Statement on Professional Ethics* also deals with the nature of the "special obligations" of the teacher. The paragraph reads as follows:

> As members of their community, professors have the rights and obligations of other citizens. Professors measure the urgency of other obligations in the light of their responsibilities to their subject, to their students, to their profession, and to their institution. When they speak or act as private persons they avoid creating the impression of speaking or acting for their college or university. As citizens engaged in a profession that depends upon freedom for its health and integrity, professors have a particular obligation to promote conditions of free inquiry and to further public understanding of academic freedom.

Both the protection of academic freedom and the requirements of academic responsibility apply not only to the full-time probationary as well as to the tenured teacher, but also to all others, such as part-time faculty and teaching assistants, who exercise teaching responsibilities.

5. The concept of "rank of full-time instructor or a higher rank" is intended to include any person who teaches a full-time load regardless of the teacher's specific title.*

6. In calling for an agreement "in writing" on the amount of credit for a faculty member's prior service at other institutions, the *Statement* furthers the general policy of full understanding by the professor of the terms and conditions of the appointment. It does not necessarily follow that a professor's tenure rights have been violated because of the absence of a written agreement on this matter. Nonetheless, especially because of the variation in permissible institutional practices, a written understanding concerning these matters at the time of appointment is particularly appropriate and advantageous to both the individual and the institution.**

---

*For a discussion of this question, see the "Report of the Special Committee on Academic Personnel Ineligible for Tenure," *AAUP Bulletin* 52 (1966): 280–82.

**For a more detailed statement on this question, see "On Crediting Prior Service Elsewhere as Part of the Probationary Period," *AAUP Bulletin* 64 (1978): 274–75.

7. The effect of this subparagraph is that a decision on tenure, favorable or unfavorable, must be made at least twelve months prior to the completion of the probationary period. If the decision is negative, the appointment for the following year becomes a terminal one. If the decision is affirmative, the provisions in the 1940 *Statement* with respect to the termination of services of teachers or investigators after the expiration of a probationary period should apply from the date when the favorable decision is made.

The general principle of notice contained in this paragraph is developed with greater specificity in the *Standards for Notice of Nonreappointment*, endorsed by the Fiftieth Annual Meeting of the American Association of University Professors (1964). These standards are:

Notice of nonreappointment, or of intention not to recommend reappointment to the governing board, should be given in writing in accordance with the following standards:

(1) *Not later than March 1 of the first academic year of service*, if the appointment expires at the end of that year; or, if a one-year appointment terminates during an academic year, at least three months in advance of its termination.

(2) *Not later than December 15 of the second academic year of service*, if the appointment expires at the end of that year; or, if an initial two-year appointment terminates during an academic year, at least six months in advance of its termination.

(3) At least twelve months before the expiration of an appointment after two or more years in the institution.

Other obligations, both of institutions and of individuals, are described in the *Statement on Recruitment and Resignation of Faculty Members*, as endorsed by the Association of American Colleges and the American Association of University Professors in 1961.

8. The freedom of probationary teachers is enhanced by the establishment of a regular procedure for the periodic evaluation and assessment of the teacher's academic performance during probationary status. Provision should be made for regularized procedures for the consideration of complaints by probationary teachers that their academic freedom has been violated. One suggested procedure to serve these purposes is contained in the *Recommended Institutional Regulations on Academic Freedom and Tenure*, prepared by the American Association of University Professors.

9. A further specification of the academic due process to which the teacher is entitled under this paragraph is contained in the *Statement on Procedural Standards in Faculty Dismissal Proceedings*, jointly approved by the American Association of University Professors and the Association of American Colleges in 1958. This interpretive document deals with the issue of suspension, about which the 1940 *Statement* is silent.

The 1958 *Statement* provides: "Suspension of the faculty member during the proceedings is justified only if immediate harm to the faculty member or others is threatened by the faculty member's continuance. Unless legal considerations forbid, any such suspension should be with pay." A suspension which is not followed by either reinstatement or the opportunity for a hearing is in effect a summary dismissal in violation of academic due process.

The concept of "moral turpitude" identifies the exceptional case in which the professor may be denied a year's teaching or pay in whole or in part. The statement applies to that kind of behavior which goes beyond simply warranting discharge and is so utterly blameworthy as to make it inappropriate to require the offering of a year's teaching or pay. The standard is not that the moral sensibilities of persons in the particular community have been affronted. The standard is behavior that would evoke condemnation by the academic community generally.

ENDORSERS

Statement on Procedural Standards in Faculty Dismissal Proceedings

---

The following statement was prepared by a joint committee representing the Association of American Colleges and the American Association of University Professors and was approved by these two associations at their annual meetings in 1958. It supplements the 1940 Statement of Principles on Academic Freedom and Tenure by providing a formulation of the "academic due process" that should be observed in dismissal proceedings. The exact procedural standards here set forth, however, "are not intended to establish a norm in the same manner as the 1940 Statement of Principles on Academic Freedom and Tenure, but are presented rather as a guide...."

The governing bodies of the American Association of University Professors and the Association of American Colleges, meeting respectively in November 1989 and January 1990, adopted several changes in language in order to remove gender-specific references from the original text.

INTRODUCTORY COMMENTS

Any approach toward settling the difficulties which have beset dismissal proceedings on many American campuses must look beyond procedure into setting and cause. A dismissal proceeding is a symptom of failure; no amount of use of removal process will help strengthen higher education as much as will the cultivation of conditions in which dismissals rarely if ever need occur.

Just as the board of control or other governing body is the legal and fiscal corporation of the college, the faculty is the academic entity. Historically, the academic corporation is the older. Faculties were formed in the Middle Ages, with managerial affairs either self-arranged or handled in course by the parent church. Modern college faculties, on the other hand, are part of a complex and extensive structure requiring legal incorporation, with stewards and managers specifically appointed to discharge certain functions.

Nonetheless, the faculty of a modern college constitutes an entity as real as that of the faculties of medieval times, in terms of collective purpose and function. A necessary precondition of a strong faculty is that it have first-hand concern with its own membership. This is properly reflected both in appointments to and in separations from the faculty body.

A well-organized institution will reflect sympathetic understanding by trustees and teachers alike of their respective and complementary roles. These should be spelled out carefully in writing and made available to all. Trustees and faculty should understand and agree on their several functions in determining who shall join and who shall remain on the faculty. One of the prime duties of the administrator is to help preserve understanding of those functions. It seems clear on the American college scene that a close positive relationship exists between the excellence of colleges, the strength of their faculties, and the extent of faculty responsibility in determining faculty membership. Such a condition is in no wise inconsistent with full faculty awareness of institutional factors with which governing boards must be primarily concerned.

In the effective college, a dismissal proceeding involving a faculty member on tenure, or one occurring during the term of an appointment, will be a rare exception, caused by individual human weakness and not by an unhealthful setting. When it does come, however, the college should be prepared for it, so that both institutional integrity and individual human rights may be preserved during the process of resolving the trouble. The faculty must be willing to recommend the dismissal of a colleague when necessary. By the same token, presidents and governing boards must be willing to give full weight to a faculty judgment favorable to a colleague.

One persistent source of difficulty is the definition of adequate cause for the dismissal of a faculty member. Despite the 1940 *Statement of Principles on Academic Freedom and Tenure* and subsequent attempts to build upon it, considerable ambiguity and misunderstanding persist throughout higher education, especially in the respective conceptions of governing boards, administrative officers, and faculties concerning this matter. The present statement assumes that individual institutions will have formulated their own definitions of adequate cause for dismissal, bearing in mind the 1940 *Statement* and standards which have developed in the experience of academic institutions.

This statement deals with procedural standards. Those recommended are not intended to establish a norm in the same manner as the 1940 *Statement of Principles on Academic Freedom and Tenure*, but are presented rather as a guide to be used according to the nature and traditions of particular institutions in giving effect to both faculty tenure rights and the obligations of faculty members in the academic community.

PROCEDURAL RECOMMENDATIONS

1. Preliminary Proceedings Concerning the Fitness of a Faculty Member

When reasons arise to question the fitness of a college or university faculty member who has tenure or whose term appointment has not expired, the appropriate administrative officers should ordinarily discuss the matter with the faculty member in personal conference. The matter may be terminated by mutual consent at this point; but if an adjustment does not result, a standing or *ad hoc* committee elected by the faculty and charged with the function of rendering confidential advice in such situations should informally inquire into the situation, to effect an adjustment if possible, and, if none is effected, to determine whether in its view formal proceedings to consider the faculty member's dismissal should be instituted. If the committee recommends that such proceedings should be begun, or if the president of the institution, even after considering a recommendation of the committee favorable to the faculty member, expresses the conviction that a proceeding should be undertaken, action should be commenced under the procedures which follow. Except where there is disagreement, a statement with reasonable particularity of the grounds proposed for the dismissal should then be jointly formulated by the president and the faculty committee; if there is disagreement, the president or the president's representative should formulate the statement.

2. Commencement of Formal Proceedings

The formal proceedings should be commenced by a communication addressed to the faculty member by the president of the institution, informing the faculty member of the statement formulated, and informing the faculty member that, at the faculty member's request, a hearing to determine whether he or she should be removed from the faculty position on the grounds stated will be conducted by a faculty committee at a specified time and place. In setting the date of the hearing, sufficient time should be allowed the faculty member to prepare a defense. The faculty member should be informed, in detail or by reference to published regulations, of the procedural rights that will be accorded. The faculty member should state in reply whether he or she wishes a hearing, and, if so, should answer in writing, not less than one week before the date set for the hearing, the statements in the president's letter.

3. Suspension of the Faculty Member

Suspension of the faculty member during the proceedings is justified only if immediate harm to the faculty member or others is threatened by the faculty member's continuance. Unless legal considerations forbid, any such suspension should be with pay.

4. Hearing Committee

The committee of faculty members to conduct the hearing and reach a decision should either be an elected standing committee not previously concerned with the case or a committee established as soon as possible after the president's letter to the faculty member has been sent. The choice of members of the hearing committee should be on the basis of their objectivity and competence and of the regard in which they are held in the academic community. The committee should elect its own chair.

5. Committee Proceeding

The committee should proceed by considering the statement of grounds for dismissal already formulated, and the faculty member's response written before the time of the hearing. If the faculty member has not requested a hearing, the committee should consider the case on the basis of the obtainable information and decide whether the faculty member should be removed; otherwise the hearing should go forward. The committee, in consultation with the president and the faculty member, should exercise its judgment as to whether the hearing should be public or private. If any facts are in dispute, the testimony of witnesses and other evidence concerning the matter set forth in the president's letter to the faculty member should be received.

The president should have the option of attendance during the hearing. The president may designate an appropriate representative to assist in developing the case; but the committee should determine the order of proof, should normally conduct the questioning of witnesses, and, if necessary, should secure the presentation of evidence important to the case.

The faculty member should have the option of assistance by counsel, whose functions should be similar to those of the representative chosen by the president. The faculty member should have the additional procedural rights set forth in the 1940 *Statement of Principles on Academic Freedom and Tenure*, and should have the aid of the committee, when needed, in securing the attendance of witnesses. The faculty member or the faculty member's counsel and the representative designated by the president should have the right, within reasonable limits, to question all witnesses who testify orally. The faculty member should have the opportunity to be confronted by all adverse witnesses. Where unusual and urgent reasons move the hearing committee to withhold this right, or where the witness cannot appear, the identity of the witness, as well as the statements of the witness, should nevertheless be disclosed to the faculty member. Subject to these safeguards, statements may when necessary be taken outside the hearing and reported to it. All of the evidence should be duly recorded. Unless special circumstances warrant, it should not be necessary to follow formal rules of court procedure.

6. Consideration by Hearing Committee

The committee should reach its decision in conference, on the basis of the hearing. Before doing so, it should give opportunity to the faculty member or the faculty member's counsel and the representative designated by the president to argue orally before it. If written briefs would be helpful, the committee may request them. The committee may proceed to decision promptly, without having the record of the hearing transcribed, where it feels that a just decision can be reached by this means; or it may await the availability of a transcript of the hearing if its decision would be aided thereby. It should make explicit findings with respect to each of the grounds of removal presented, and a reasoned opinion may be desirable. Publicity concerning the committee's decision may properly be withheld until consideration has been given to the case by the governing body of the institution. The president and the faculty member should be notified of the decision in writing and should be given a copy of the record of the hearing. Any release to the public should be made through the president's office.

7. Consideration by Governing Body

The president should transmit to the governing body the full report of the hearing committee, stating its action. On the assumption that the governing board has accepted the principle of the faculty hearing committee, acceptance of the committee's decision would normally be expected. If the governing body chooses to review the case, its review should be based on the record of the previous hearing, accompanied by opportunity for argument, oral or written or both, by the principals at the hearing or their representatives. The decision of the hearing committee should either be sustained or the proceeding be returned to the committee with objections specified. In such a case the committee should reconsider, taking account of the stated objections and receiving new evidence if necessary. It should frame its decision and communicate it in the same manner as before. Only after study of the committee's reconsideration should the governing body make a final decision overruling the committee.

8. Publicity

Except for such simple announcements as may be required, covering the time of the hearing and similar matters, public statements about the case by either the faculty member or administrative officers should be avoided so far as possible until the proceedings have been completed. Announcement of the final decision should include a statement of the hearing committee's original action, if this has not previously been made known.

Statement on Procedural Standards in the Renewal or Nonrenewal of Faculty Appointments

The statement which follows, a revision of a statement originally adopted in 1971, was approved by Committee A on Academic Freedom and Tenure, adopted by the Council as Association policy in November 1989, and endorsed by the Seventy-sixth Annual Meeting.

Except for special appointments clearly designated at the outset as involving only a brief association with the institution, all full-time faculty appointments are either with continuous tenure or probationary for tenure. Procedures bearing on the renewal or nonrenewal of probationary appointments are this statement's concern.

THE PROBATIONARY PERIOD: STANDARDS AND CRITERIA

The 1940 *Statement of Principles on Academic Freedom and Tenure* prescribes that "during the probationary period a teacher should have the academic freedom that all other members of the faculty have." The Association's *Recommended Institutional Regulations on Academic Freedom and Tenure* prescribe further that "all members of the faculty, whether tenured or not, are entitled to protection against illegal or unconstitutional discrimination by the institution, or discrimination on a basis not demonstrably related to the faculty member's professional performance...." A number of the rights of nontenured faculty members provide support for their academic freedom and protection against improper discrimination. They cannot, for example, be dismissed before the end of a term appointment except for adequate cause that has been demonstrated through academic due process—a right they share with tenured members of the faculty. If they assert that they have been given notice of nonreappointment in violation of academic freedom or because of improper discrimination, they are entitled to an opportunity to establish their claim in accordance with Regulation 10 of the *Recommended Institutional Regulations*. They are entitled to timely notice of nonreappointment in accordance with the schedule prescribed in the statement on *Standards for Notice of Nonreappointment*.[1]

Lacking the reinforcement of tenure, however, academic freedom and protection against improper discrimination for probationary faculty members have depended primarily upon the understanding and support of their tenured colleagues, the administration, and professional organizations, especially the Association. In the joint *Statement on Government of Colleges and Universities*, the Association and the other sponsoring organizations have asserted that "faculty status and related matters are primarily a faculty responsibility; this area includes appointments,

[1]The *Standards for Notice* are as follows:
1. *Not later than March 1 of the first academic year of service*, if the appointment expires at the end of that year; or, if a one-year appointment terminates during an academic year, at least three months in advance of its termination;
2. *Not later than December 15 of the second academic year of service*, if the appointment expires at the end of that year; or, if an initial two-year appointment terminates during an academic year, at least six months in advance of its termination;
3. At least twelve months before the expiration of an appointment after two or more years in the institution.

reappointments, decisions not to reappoint, promotions, the granting of tenure, and dismissal.'' Collegial deliberation of the kind envisioned by the *Statement on Government* will minimize the risk of a violation of academic freedom, of improper discrimination, and of a decision that is arbitrary or based on inadequate consideration.

Frequently, young faculty members have had no training or experience in teaching, and their first major research endeavor may still be uncompleted at the time they start their careers as college teachers. Under these circumstances, it is particularly important that there be a probationary period—a maximum of seven years under the 1940 *Statement of Principles on Academic Freedom and Tenure*—before tenure is granted. Such a period gives probationary faculty members time to prove themselves, and their colleagues time to observe and evaluate them on the basis of their performance in the position rather than on the basis only of their education, training, and recommendations.

Good practice requires that the institution (department, college, or university) define its criteria for reappointment and tenure and its procedures for reaching decisions on these matters. The 1940 *Statement of Principles* prescribes that "the precise terms and conditions of every appointment should be stated in writing and be in the possession of both institution and teacher before the appointment is consummated." Moreover, fairness to probationary faculty members prescribes that they be informed, early in their appointments, of the substantive and procedural standards that will be followed in determining whether or not their appointments will be renewed or tenure will be granted.

The Association accordingly recommends:

1. *Criteria and Notice of Standards.* Probationary faculty members should be advised, early in their appointment, of the substantive and procedural standards generally accepted in decisions affecting renewal and tenure. Any special standards adopted by their particular departments or schools should also be brought to their attention.

THE PROBATIONARY PERIOD: EVALUATION AND DECISION

The relationship of the senior and junior faculty should be one of colleagueship, even though nontenured faculty members know that in time they will be judged by their senior colleagues. Thus the procedures adopted for evaluation and possible notification of nonrenewal should not endanger this relationship where it exists, and should encourage it where it does not. Nontenured faculty members should have available to them the advice and assistance of their senior colleagues; and the ability of senior colleagues to make a sound decision on renewal or tenure will be enhanced if an opportunity is provided for a regular review of the candidate's qualifications. A conjunction of the roles in counseling and evaluation may be productive: for example, an evaluation, whether interim or at the time of final determination of renewal or tenure, should be presented in such a manner as to assist nontenured faculty members as they strive to improve their performance.

Any recommendation regarding renewal or tenure should be reached by an appropriate faculty group in accordance with procedures approved by the faculty. Because it is important to both the faculty member and the decision-making body that all significant information be considered, the candidate should be notified that a decision is to be made regarding renewal of appointment or the granting of tenure and should be afforded an opportunity to submit material that the candidate believes to be relevant to the decision.

The Association accordingly recommends:

2. (a) *Periodic Review.* There should be provision for periodic review of a faculty member's situation during the probationary service.
   (b) *Opportunity to Submit Material.* Probationary faculty members should be advised of the time when decisions affecting renewal and tenure are ordinarily made, and they should be given the opportunity to submit material that they believe will be helpful to an adequate consideration of their circumstances.

Observance of the practices and procedures outlined above should minimize the likelihood of reasonable complaint if nontenured faculty members are given notice of nonreappointment. They will have been informed of the criteria and procedures for renewal and tenure; they will have been counseled by faculty colleagues; they will have been given an opportunity to have all material relevant to their evaluation considered; and they will have a timely decision representing the views of faculty colleagues.

NOTICE OF REASONS

Since 1971 it has been the Association's position, reached after careful examination of advantages and disadvantages, that nontenured faculty members notified of nonreappointment should, upon request, receive a statement of the reasons for the decision. In reaching this position, the Association considered the needs both of the institution and of the individual faculty member.

A major responsibility of the institution is to recruit and retain the best qualified faculty within its goals and means. In a matter of such fundamental importance, the institution, through the appropriate faculty agencies, must be accorded the widest latitude consistent with academic freedom, equal opportunity, and the standards of fairness. The Association recognized that the requirement of giving reasons could lead, however erroneously, to an expectation that the decision-making body must justify its decision. A notice of nonreappointment could thus become confused with dismissal for cause, and under these circumstances the decision-making body could become reluctant to reach adverse decisions which could culminate in grievance procedures. As a result there was some risk that the important distinction between tenure and probation would be eroded.

Weighed against these important institutional concerns, however, were the interests of the individual faculty members. They could be honestly unaware of the reasons for a negative decision, and the decision could be based on a judgment of shortcomings which they could easily remedy if informed of them. A decision not to renew an appointment could be based on erroneous information which the faculty member could readily correct if informed of the basis for the decision. Again, the decision could be based on considerations of institutional policy or program development which have nothing to do with the faculty member's professional competence, and if not informed of the reasons the faculty member could mistakenly assume that a judgment of inadequate performance has been made. In the face of a persistent refusal to supply the reasons, a faculty member may be more inclined to attribute improper motivations to the decision-making body or to conclude that its evaluation has been based upon inadequate consideration. If the faculty member wished to request a reconsideration of the decision, or a review by another body, ignorance of the reasons for the decision would create difficulties both in reaching a decision whether to initiate such a request and in presenting a case for reconsideration or review.

The Association's extensive experience with specific cases since 1971 has confirmed its conclusion that the reasons in support of the faculty member's right to be informed outweigh the countervailing risks. Every notice of nonreappointment, however, need not be accompanied by a written statement of the reasons for nonreappointment. It may not always be to the advantage of the faculty member to be informed of the reasons for nonreappointment, particularly in writing. The faculty member may be placed under obligation to divulge them to the appointing body of another institution if it inquired. Similarly, a written record is likely to become the basis for continuing responses by the faculty member's former institution to prospective appointing bodies.

At many institutions, moreover, the procedures of evaluation and decision may make it difficult, if not impossible, to compile a statement of reasons which precisely reflects the basis of the decision. When a number of faculty members participate in the decision, they may oppose a reappointment for a variety of reasons, few or none of which may represent a majority view. To include every reason, no matter how few have held it, in a written statement to the faculty member may misrepresent the general view and damage unnecessarily both the morale and the professional future of the faculty member.

In many situations, of course, a decision not to reappoint will not reflect adversely upon the faculty member. An institution may, for example, find it necessary for financial or other reasons to restrict its offerings in a given department. The acquisition of tenure may depend not only upon satisfactory performance but also upon a long-term opening. Nonrenewal in these cases does not suggest a serious adverse judgment. In these situations, providing a statement of reasons, either written or oral, should pose no difficulty, and such a statement may in fact assist the faculty member in searching for a new position.

Should the faculty member, after weighing the considerations cited above, decide to request the reasons for the decision against reappointment, the reasons should be given. The faculty member also should have the opportunity to request a reconsideration by the decision-making body.

The Association accordingly recommends:

3. *Notice of Reasons*. In the event of a decision not to renew an appointment, the faculty member should be informed of the decision in writing, and, upon request, be advised of the reasons which contributed to that decision. The faculty member should also have the opportunity to request a reconsideration by the decision-making body.

WRITTEN REASONS

Having been given orally the reasons which contributed to the decision against reappointment, the faculty member, to avoid misunderstanding, may request that they be confirmed in writing. The faculty member may wish to petition the appropriate faculty committee, in accordance with Regulation 10 of the Association's *Recommended Institutional Regulations*, to consider an allegation that the reasons given, or that other reasons which were not stated, constitute a violation of academic freedom or improper discrimination. The faculty member may wish to petition a committee, in accordance with Regulation 15 of the *Recommended Institutional Regulations*, to consider a complaint that the decision resulted from inadequate consideration and was therefore unfair. The faculty member may believe that a written statement of reasons may be useful in pursuing a professional career.

If the department chair or other appropriate institutional officer to whom the request is made believes that confirming the oral statement in writing may be damaging to the faculty member on grounds such as those cited earlier in this statement, it would be desirable for that officer to explain the possible adverse consequences of confirming the oral statement in writing. If in spite of this explanation the faculty member continues to request a written statement, the request should be honored.

The Association accordingly recommends:

4. *Written Reasons*. If the faculty member expresses a desire to petition the grievance committee (such as is described in Regulations 10 and 15 of the Association's *Recommended Institutional Regulations*), or any other appropriate committee, to use its good offices of inquiry, recommendation, and report, or if the request is made for any other reason satisfactory to the faculty member alone, the reasons given in explanation of the nonrenewal should be confirmed in writing.

REVIEW PROCEDURES: ALLEGATIONS OF VIOLATION OF ACADEMIC FREEDOM OR OF DISCRIMINATION

The best safeguard against a proliferation of grievance petitions on a given campus is the observance of sound principles and procedures of academic freedom and tenure and of institutional government. Observance of the procedures recommended in this statement—procedures which would provide guidance to nontenured faculty members, help assure them of a fair professional evaluation, and enlighten them concerning the reasons contributing to key decisions of their colleagues—should contribute to the achievement of harmonious faculty relationships and the development of well-qualified faculties.

Even with the best practices and procedures, however, faculty members will at times think that they have been improperly or unjustly treated and may wish another faculty group to review a decision of the faculty body immediately involved. The Association believes that fairness to both the individual and the institution requires that the institution provide for such a review when it is requested. The possibility of a violation of academic freedom or of improper discrimination is of vital concern to the institution as a whole, and where either is alleged it is of cardinal importance to the faculty and the administration to determine whether substantial grounds for the allegation exist. The institution should also be concerned to see that decisions respecting reappointment are based upon adequate consideration, and provision should thus be made for a review of allegations by affected faculty members that the consideration has been inadequate.

Because of the broader significance of a violation of academic freedom or of improper discrimination, the Association believes that the procedures to be followed in these two kinds of complaints should be kept separate from a complaint over adequacy of consideration. Regulation 10 of the *Recommended Institutional Regulations* provides a specific procedure for the review of complaints of academic freedom violation or of discrimination.[2]

If a faculty member on probationary or other nontenured appointment alleges that a decision against reappointment was based significantly on considerations violative of (1) academic freedom or (2) governing policies on making appointments without prejudice with respect to race, sex, religion, national origin, age, physical handicap, marital status, or sexual or affectional preference, the allegation will be given preliminary consideration by the [insert name of committee], which will seek to settle the matter by informal methods. The allegation will be accompanied by a statement that the faculty member agrees to the presentation, for the consideration of the faculty committees, of such reasons and evidence as the institution may allege in support of its decision. If the difficulty is unresolved at this stage, and if the committee so recommends, the matter will be heard in the manner set forth in Regulations 5 and 6, except that the faculty member making the complaint is responsible for stating the grounds upon which the allegations are based, and the burden of proof will rest upon the faculty member. If the faculty member succeeds in establishing a *prima facie* case, it is incumbent upon those who made the decision against reappointment to come forward with evidence in support of their decision. Statistical evidence of improper discrimination may be used in establishing a *prima facie* case.

The Association accordingly recommends:

5. *Petition for Review Alleging an Academic Freedom Violation or Improper Discrimination.* Insofar as the petition for review alleges a violation of academic freedom or improper discrimination, the functions of the committee that reviews the faculty member's petition should be the following:
   (a) To determine whether or not the notice of nonreappointment constitutes on its face a violation of academic freedom or improper discrimination.
   (b) To seek to settle the matter by informal methods.
   (c) If the matter remains unresolved, to decide whether or not the evidence submitted in support of the petition warrants a recommendation that a formal proceeding be conducted in accordance with Regulations 5 and 6 of the *Recommended Institutional Regulations*, with the burden of proof resting upon the complaining faculty member.

REVIEW PROCEDURES: ALLEGATIONS OF INADEQUATE CONSIDERATION

Complaints of inadequate consideration are likely to relate to matters of professional judgment, where the department or departmental agency should have primary authority. For this reason, the basic functions of the review committee should be to determine whether the appropriate faculty body gave adequate consideration to the faculty member's candidacy in reaching its decision and, if the review committee determines otherwise, to request reconsideration by that body.

---

[2]Faculties processing complaints under Regulations 10 and 15 may wish to secure the further advice of the Association's Washington office.

It is easier to state what the standard "adequate consideration" does not mean than to specify in detail what it does. It does not mean that the review committee should substitute its own judgment for that of members of the department on the merits of whether the candidate should be reappointed or given tenure. The conscientious judgment of the candidate's departmental colleagues must prevail if the invaluable tradition of departmental autonomy in professional judgments is to prevail. The term "adequate consideration" refers essentially to procedural rather than substantive issues: Was the decision conscientiously arrived at? Was all available evidence bearing on the relevant performance of the candidate sought out and considered? Was there adequate deliberation by the department over the import of the evidence in the light of the relevant standards? Were irrelevant and improper standards excluded from consideration? Was the decision a *bona fide* exercise of professional academic judgment? These are the kinds of questions suggested by the standard "adequate consideration."

If in applying this standard the review committee concludes that adequate consideration was not given, its appropriate response should be to recommend to the department that it assess the merits once again, this time remedying the inadequacies of its prior consideration.

An acceptable review procedure, representing one procedural system within which such judgments may be made, is outlined in Regulation 15 of the *Recommended Institutional Regulations*, as follows:

> If any faculty member alleges cause for grievance in any matter not covered by the procedures described in the foregoing regulations, the faculty member may petition the elected faculty grievance committee [here name the committee] for redress. The petition will set forth in detail the nature of the grievance and will state against whom the grievance is directed. It will contain any factual or other data which the petitioner deems pertinent to the case. Statistical evidence of improper discrimination, including discrimination in salary, may be used in establishing a *prima facie* case. The committee will decide whether or not the facts merit a detailed investigation; if the faculty member succeeds in establishing a *prima facie* case, it is incumbent upon those who made the decision to come forward with evidence in support of their decision. Submission of a petition will not automatically entail investigation or detailed consideration thereof. The committee may seek to bring about a settlement of the issue satisfactory to the parties. If in the opinion of the committee such a settlement is not possible or is not appropriate, the committee will report its findings and recommendations to the petitioner and to the appropriate administrative officer and faculty body, and the petitioner will, upon request, be provided an opportunity to present the grievance to them. The grievance committee will consist of three [or some other number] elected members of the faculty. No officer of administration will serve on the committee.

The Association accordingly recommends:

6. *Petition for Review Alleging Inadequate Consideration.* Insofar as the petition for review alleges inadequate consideration, the functions of the committee which reviews the faculty member's petition should be the following:
   (a) to determine whether the decision of the appropriate faculty body was the result of adequate consideration, with the understanding that the review committee should not substitute its judgment on the merits for that of the faculty body;
   (b) to request reconsideration by the faculty body when the committee believes that adequate consideration was not given to the faculty member's qualifications (in such instances, the committee should indicate the respects in which it believes that consideration may have been inadequate);
   (c) to provide copies of its report and recommendation to the faculty member, the faculty body, and the president or other appropriate administrative officer.

Recommended Institutional Regulations on Academic Freedom and Tenure

---

Recommended Institutional Regulations on Academic Freedom and Tenure set forth, in language suitable for use by an institution of higher education, rules which derive from the chief provisions and interpretations of the 1940 Statement of Principles on Academic Freedom and Tenure and of the 1958 Statement on Procedural Standards in Faculty Dismissal Proceedings. The Recommended Institutional Regulations were first formulated by Committee A on Academic Freedom and Tenure in 1957. A revised and expanded text, approved by Committee A in 1968, reflected the development of Association standards and procedures as set forth in the 1961 Statement on Recruitment and Resignation of Faculty Members, the 1964 Statement on the Standards for Notice of Nonreappointment, and the 1966 Statement on Government of Colleges and Universities. Texts with further revisions were approved by Committee A in 1972 and again in 1976.

The current revision, approved by Committee A in 1982, is based upon the Association's continuing experience in evaluating regulations actually in force at particular institutions. The 1982 revision is also based upon further definition of the standards and procedures of the Association as set forth in the 1970 Interpretive Comments of the 1940 Statement of Principles, the 1971 Council Statement on Freedom and Responsibility, the 1971 Statement on Procedural Standards in the Renewal or Nonrenewal of Faculty Appointments, the 1972 Statement of Principles on Leaves of Absence, recommended procedure adopted by the Council in 1976 on Termination of Faculty Appointments Because of Financial Exigency, Discontinuance of a Program or Department, or Medical Reasons, the 1976 policy On Discrimination, and the 1977 statement On Processing Complaints of Discrimination on the Basis of Sex. The Association will be glad to assist in interpretation of the regulations or to consult about their incorporation in, or adaptation to, the rules of a particular college or university.

FOREWORD

These regulations are designed to enable the [named institution] to protect academic freedom and tenure and to ensure academic due process. The principles implicit in these regulations are for the benefit of all who are involved with or are affected by the policies and programs of the institution. A college or university is a marketplace of ideas, and it cannot fulfill its purposes of transmitting, evaluating, and extending knowledge if it requires conformity with any orthodoxy of content and method. In the words of the United States Supreme Court, "Teachers and students must always remain free to inquire, to study and to evaluate, to gain new maturity and understanding; otherwise our civilization will stagnate and die."

1. STATEMENT OF TERMS OF APPOINTMENT

(a) The terms and conditions of every appointment to the faculty will be stated or confirmed in writing, and a copy of the appointment document will be supplied to the faculty member.

Any subsequent extensions or modifications of an appointment, and any special understandings, or any notices incumbent upon either party to provide, will be stated or confirmed in writing and a copy will be given to the faculty member.

(b) With the exception of special appointments clearly limited to a brief association with the institution, and reappointments of retired faculty members on special conditions, all full-time faculty appointments are of two kinds: (1) probationary appointments; (2) appointments with continuous tenure.

(c) Except for faculty members who have tenure status, every person with a teaching or research appointment of any kind will be informed each year in writing of the appointment and of all matters relative to eligibility for the acquisition of tenure.

2. PROBATIONARY APPOINTMENTS

(a) Probationary appointments may be for one year, or for other stated periods, subject to renewal. The total period of full-time service prior to the acquisition of continuous tenure will not exceed ____ years,[1] including all previous full-time service with the rank of instructor or higher in other institutions of higher learning [*except* that the probationary period may extend to as much as four years, even if the total full-time service in the profession thereby exceeds seven years; the terms of such extension will be stated in writing at the time of initial appointment].[2] Scholarly leave of absence for one year or less will count as part of the probationary period as if it were prior service at another institution, unless the individual and the institution agree in writing to an exception to this provision at the time the leave is granted.

(b) The faculty member will be advised, at the time of initial appointment, of the substantive standards and procedures generally employed in decisions affecting renewal and tenure. Any special standards adopted by the faculty member's department or school will also be transmitted. The faculty member will be advised of the time when decisions affecting renewal or tenure are ordinarily made, and will be given the opportunity to submit material believed to be helpful to an adequate consideration of the faculty member's circumstances.

(c) Regardless of the stated term or other provisions of any appointments, written notice that a probationary appointment is not to be renewed will be given to the faculty member in advance of the expiration of the appointment, as follows: (1) not later than March 1 of the first academic year of service if the appointment expires at the end of that year; or, if a one-year appointment terminates during an academic year, at least three months in advance of its termination; (2) not later than December 15 of the second academic year of service if the appointment expires at the end of that year; or, if an initial two-year appointment terminates during an academic year, at least six months in advance of its termination; (3) at least twelve months before the expiration of an appointment after two or more years of service at the institution. The institution will normally notify faculty members of the terms and conditions of their renewals by March 15, but in no case will such information be given later than _____.[3]

(d) When a faculty recommendation or a decision not to renew an appointment has first been reached, the faculty member involved will be informed of that recommendation or decision in writing by the body or individual making the initial recommendation or decision; the faculty member will be advised upon request of the reasons which contributed to that decision. The faculty member may request a reconsideration by the recommending or deciding body.

(e) If the faculty member so requests, the reasons given in explanation of the nonrenewal will be confirmed in writing.

[1] Under the 1940 *Statement of Principles on Academic Freedom and Tenure*, this period may not exceed seven years.
[2] The exception here noted applies only to an institution whose maximum probationary period exceeds four years.
[3] April 15 is the recommended date.

(f) Insofar as the faculty member alleges that the decision against renewal by the appropriate faculty body was based on inadequate consideration, the committee[4] which reviews the faculty member's allegation will determine whether the decision was the result of adequate consideration in terms of the relevant standards of the institution. The review committee will not substitute its judgment on the merits for that of the faculty body. If the review committee believes that adequate consideration was not given to the faculty member's qualifications, it will request reconsideration by the faculty body, indicating the respects in which it believes the consideration may have been inadequate. It will provide copies of its findings to the faculty member, the faculty body, and the president or other appropriate administrative officer.

3. TERMINATION OF APPOINTMENT BY FACULTY MEMBERS

Faculty members may terminate their appointments effective at the end of an academic year, provided that they give notice in writing at the earliest possible opportunity, but not later than May 15, or thirty days after receiving notification of the terms of appointment for the coming year, whichever date occurs later. Faculty members may properly request a waiver of this requirement of notice in case of hardship or in a situation where they would otherwise be denied substantial professional advancement or other opportunity.

4. TERMINATION OF APPOINTMENTS BY THE INSTITUTION

(a) Termination of an appointment with continuous tenure, or of a probationary or special appointment before the end of the specified term, may be effected by the institution only for adequate cause.

(b) If termination takes the form of a dismissal for cause, it will be pursuant to the procedure specified in Regulation 5.

Financial Exigency

(c) (1) Termination of an appointment with continuous tenure, or of a probationary or special appointment before the end of the specified term, may occur under extraordinary circumstances because of a demonstrably *bona fide* financial exigency, i.e., an imminent financial crisis which threatens the survival of the institution as a whole and which cannot be alleviated by less drastic means.

[NOTE: Each institution in adopting regulations on financial exigency will need to decide how to share and allocate the hard judgments and decisions that are necessary in such a crisis.

As a first step, there should be a faculty body which participates in the decision that a condition of financial exigency exists or is imminent,[5] and that all feasible alternatives to termination of appointments have been pursued.

[4]This committee, which can be the grievance committee noted in Regulation 15, is to be an elected faculty body. Similarly, the members of the committees noted in Regulations 4(c)(2), 4(d)(3), and 10 are to be elected. A committee of faculty members appointed by an appropriate elected faculty body can substitute for a committee that is elected directly. [Preceding note adopted by Committee A in June 1990.]

[5]See "The Role of the Faculty in Budgetary and Salary Matters" (*AAUP Bulletin* 62 [1976]: 379–81), and especially the following passages:

The faculty should participate both in the preparation of the total institutional budget and (within the framework of the total budget) in decisions relevant to the further apportioning of its specific fiscal divisions (salaries, academic programs, tuition, physical plant and grounds, etc.). The soundness of resulting decisions should be enhanced if an elected representative committee of the faculty participates in deciding on the overall allocation of institutional resources and the proportion to be devoted directly to the academic program. This committee should be given access to all information that it requires to perform its task effectively, and it should have the opportunity to confer periodically with representatives of the administration and governing board....

Judgments determining where within the overall academic program termination of appointments may occur involve considerations of educational policy, including affirmative action, as well as of faculty status, and should therefore be the primary responsibility of the faculty or of an appropriate faculty body.[6] The faculty or an appropriate faculty body should also exercise primary responsibility in determining the criteria for identifying the individuals whose appointments are to be terminated. These criteria may appropriately include considerations of length of service.

The responsibility for identifying individuals whose appointments are to be terminated should be committed to a person or group designated or approved by the faculty. The allocation of this responsibility may vary according to the size and character of the institution, the extent of the terminations to be made, or other considerations of fairness in judgment. The case of a faculty member given notice of proposed termination of appointment will be governed by the following procedure.]

(2) If the administration issues notice to a particular faculty member of an intention to terminate the appointment because of financial exigency, the faculty member will have the right to a full hearing before a faculty committee. The hearing need not conform in all respects with a proceeding conducted pursuant to Regulation 5, but the essentials of an on-the-record adjudicative hearing will be observed. The issues in this hearing may include:

(i) The existence and extent of the condition of financial exigency. The burden will rest on the administration to prove the existence and extent of the condition. The findings of a faculty committee in a previous proceeding involving the same issue may be introduced.

(ii) The validity of the educational judgments and the criteria for identification for termination; but the recommendations of a faculty body on these matters will be considered presumptively valid.

(iii) Whether the criteria are being properly applied in the individual case.

(3) If the institution, because of financial exigency, terminates appointments, it will not at the same time make new appointments except in extraordinary circumstances where a serious distortion in the academic program would otherwise result. The appointment of a faculty member with tenure will not be terminated in favor of retaining a faculty member without tenure, except in extraordinary circumstances where a serious distortion of the academic program would otherwise result.

(4) Before terminating an appointment because of financial exigency, the institution, with faculty participation, will make every effort to place the faculty member concerned in another suitable position within the institution.

(5) In all cases of termination of appointment because of financial exigency, the faculty member concerned will be given notice or severance salary not less than as prescribed in Regulation 8.

(6) In all cases of termination of appointment because of financial exigency, the place of the faculty member concerned will not be filled by a replacement within a period of three years,

---

Circumstances of financial exigency obviously pose special problems. At institutions experiencing major threats to their continued financial support, the faculty should be informed as early and specifically as possible of significant impending financial difficulties. The faculty—with substantial representation from its nontenured as well as its tenured members, since it is the former who are likely to bear the brunt of the reduction—should participate at the department, college or professional school, and institutionwide levels in key decisions as to the future of the institution and of specific academic programs within the institution. The faculty, employing accepted standards of due process, should assume primary responsibility for determining the status of individual faculty members.

[6] See "Joint Statement on Government of Colleges and Universities" (*Academe* 76 [May–June 1990]: 45–48), and especially the following passage:

Faculty status and related matters are primarily a faculty responsibility; this area includes appointments, reappointments, decisions not to reappoint, promotions, the granting of tenure, and dismissal. The primary responsibility of the faculty for such matters is based upon the fact that its judgment is central to general educational policy.

unless the released faculty member has been offered reinstatement and a reasonable time in which to accept or decline it.

Discontinuance of Program or Department Not Mandated by Financial Exigency[7]

(d) Termination of an appointment with continuous tenure, or of a probationary or special appointment before the end of the specified term, may occur as a result of *bona fide* formal discontinuance of a program or department of instruction. The following standards and procedures will apply.

    (1) The decision to discontinue formally a program or department of instruction will be based essentially upon educational considerations, as determined primarily by the faculty as a whole or an appropriate committee thereof.

       [NOTE: "Educational considerations" do not include cyclical or temporary variations in enrollment. They must reflect long-range judgments that the educational mission of the institution as a whole will be enhanced by the discontinuance.]

    (2) Before the administration issues notice to a faculty member of its intention to terminate an appointment because of formal discontinuance of a program or department of instruction, the institution will make every effort to place the faculty member concerned in another suitable position. If placement in another position would be facilitated by a reasonable period of training, financial and other support for such training will be proffered. If no position is available within the institution, with or without retraining, the faculty member's appointment then may be terminated, but only with provision for severance salary equitably adjusted to the faculty member's length of past and potential service.

       [NOTE: When an institution proposes to discontinue a program or department of instruction, it should plan to bear the costs of relocating, training, or otherwise compensating faculty members adversely affected.]

    (3) A faculty member may appeal a proposed relocation or termination resulting from a discontinuance and has a right to a full hearing before a faculty committee. The hearing need not conform in all respects with a proceeding conducted pursuant to Regulation 5, but the essentials of an on-the-record adjudicative hearing will be observed. The issues in such a hearing may include the institution's failure to satisfy any of the conditions specified in Regulation 4(d). In such a hearing a faculty determination that a program or department is to be discontinued will be considered presumptively valid, but the burden of proof on other issues will rest on the administration.

Termination for Medical Reasons

(e) Termination of an appointment with tenure, or of a probationary or special appointment before the end of the period of appointment, for medical reasons, will be based upon clear and convincing medical evidence that the faculty member cannot continue to fulfill the terms and conditions of the appointment. The decision to terminate will be reached only after there has been appropriate consultation and after the faculty member concerned, or someone representing the faculty member, has been informed of the basis of the proposed action and has been afforded an opportunity to present the faculty member's position and to respond to the evidence. If the faculty member so requests, the evidence will be reviewed by the Faculty Committee on Academic Freedom and Tenure [or whatever title it may have] before a final decision is made by the governing board on the recommendation of the administration. The faculty member will be given severance salary not less than as prescribed in Regulation 8.

Review

(f) In cases of termination of appointment, the governing board will be available for ultimate review.

---

[7]When discontinuance of a program or department is mandated by financial exigency of the institution, the standards of Regulation 4(c) above will apply.

5. DISMISSAL PROCEDURES

(a) Adequate cause for a dismissal will be related, directly and substantially, to the fitness of faculty members in their professional capacities as teachers or researchers. Dismissal will not be used to restrain faculty members in their exercise of academic freedom or other rights of American citizens.

(b) Dismissal of a faculty member with continuous tenure, or with a special or probationary appointment before the end of the specified term, will be preceded by: (1) discussions between the faculty member and appropriate administrative officers looking toward a mutual settlement; (2) informal inquiry by the duly elected faculty committee [insert name of committee] which may, failing to effect an adjustment, determine whether in its opinion dismissal proceedings should be undertaken, without its opinion being binding upon the president; (3) a statement of charges, framed with reasonable particularity by the president or the president's delegate.

(c) A dismissal, as defined in Regulation 5(a), will be preceded by a statement of reasons, and the individual concerned will have the right to be heard initially by the elected faculty hearing committee [insert name of committee].[8] Members deeming themselves disqualified for bias or interest will remove themselves from the case, either at the request of a party or on their own initiative. Each party will have a maximum of two challenges without stated cause.[9]

   (1) Pending a final decision by the hearing committee, the faculty member will be suspended, or assigned to other duties in lieu of suspension, only if immediate harm to the faculty member or others is threatened by continuance. Before suspending a faculty member, pending an ultimate determination of the faculty member's status through the institution's hearing procedures, the administration will consult with the Faculty Committee on Academic Freedom and Tenure [or whatever other title it may have] concerning the propriety, the length, and the other conditions of the suspension. A suspension which is intended to be final is a dismissal, and will be treated as such. Salary will continue during the period of the suspension.

   (2) The hearing committee may, with the consent of the parties concerned, hold joint prehearing meetings with the parties in order to (i) simplify the issues, (ii) effect stipulations of facts, (iii) provide for the exchange of documentary or other information, and (iv) achieve such other appropriate prehearing objectives as will make the hearing fair, effective, and expeditious.

   (3) Service of notice of hearing with specific charges in writing will be made at least twenty days prior to the hearing. The faculty member may waive a hearing or may respond to the charges in writing at any time before the hearing. If the faculty member waives a hearing, but denies the charges or asserts that the charges do not support a finding of adequate cause, the hearing tribunal will evaluate all available evidence and rest its recommendation upon the evidence in the record.

   (4) The committee, in consultation with the president and the faculty member, will exercise its judgment as to whether the hearing should be public or private.

   (5) During the proceedings the faculty member will be permitted to have an academic advisor and counsel of the faculty member's choice.

   (6) At the request of either party or the hearing committee, a representative of a responsible educational association will be permitted to attend the proceedings as an observer.

   (7) A verbatim record of the hearing or hearings will be taken and a typewritten copy will be made available to the faculty member without cost, at the faculty member's request.

---

[8]This committee should not be the same as the committee referred to in Regulation 5(b)(2).

[9]Regulations of the institution should provide for alternates, or for some other method of filling vacancies on the hearing committee resulting from disqualification, challenge without stated cause, illness, resignation, or other reason.

(8) The burden of proof that adequate cause exists rests with the institution and will be satisfied only by clear and convincing evidence in the record considered as a whole.

(9) The hearing committee will grant adjournments to enable either party to investigate evidence as to which a valid claim of surprise is made.

(10) The faculty member will be afforded an opportunity to obtain necessary witnesses and documentary or other evidence. The administration will cooperate with the hearing committee in securing witnesses and making available documentary and other evidence.

(11) The faculty member and the administration will have the right to confront and cross-examine all witnesses. Where the witnesses cannot or will not appear, but the committee determines that the interests of justice require admission of their statements, the committee will identify the witnesses, disclose their statements, and if possible provide for interrogatories.

(12) In the hearing of charges of incompetence, the testimony will include that of qualified faculty members from this or other institutions of higher education.

(13) The hearing committee will not be bound by strict rules of legal evidence, and may admit any evidence which is of probative value in determining the issues involved. Every possible effort will be made to obtain the most reliable evidence available.

(14) The findings of fact and the decision will be based solely on the hearing record.

(15) Except for such simple announcements as may be required, covering the time of the hearing and similar matters, public statements and publicity about the case by either the faculty member or administrative officers will be avoided so far as possible until the proceedings have been completed, including consideration by the governing board of the institution. The president and the faculty member will be notified of the decision in writing and will be given a copy of the record of the hearing.

(16) If the hearing committee concludes that adequate cause for dismissal has not been established by the evidence in the record, it will so report to the president. If the president rejects the report, the president will state the reasons for doing so, in writing, to the hearing committee and to the faculty member, and provide an opportunity for response before transmitting the case to the governing board. If the hearing committee concludes that adequate cause for a dismissal has been established, but that an academic penalty less than dismissal would be more appropriate, it will so recommend, with supporting reasons.

6. ACTION BY THE GOVERNING BOARD

If dismissal or other severe sanction is recommended, the president will, on request of the faculty member, transmit to the governing board the record of the case. The governing board's review will be based on the record of the committee hearing, and it will provide opportunity for argument, oral or written or both, by the principals at the hearings or by their representatives. The decision of the hearing committee will either be sustained or the proceeding returned to the committee with specific objections. The committee will then reconsider, taking into account the stated objections and receiving new evidence if necessary. The governing board will make a final decision only after study of the committee's reconsideration.

7. PROCEDURES FOR IMPOSITION OF SANCTIONS OTHER THAN DISMISSAL

(a) If the administration believes that the conduct of a faculty member, although not constituting adequate cause for dismissal, is sufficiently grave to justify imposition of a severe sanction, such as suspension from service for a stated period, the administration may institute a proceeding to impose such a severe sanction; the procedures outlined in Regulation 5 will govern such a proceeding.

(b) If the administration believes that the conduct of a faculty member justifies imposition of a minor sanction, such as a reprimand, it will notify the faculty member of the basis of the proposed sanction and provide the faculty member with an opportunity to persuade the administration that the proposed sanction should not be imposed. A faculty member who believes that a major sanction has been incorrectly imposed under this paragraph, or that a minor sanction has been unjustly imposed, may, pursuant to Regulation 15, petition the faculty grievance committee for such action as may be appropriate.

8. TERMINAL SALARY OR NOTICE

If the appointment is terminated, the faculty member will receive salary or notice in accordance with the following schedule: at least three months, if the final decision is reached by March 1 (or three months prior to the expiration) of the first year of probationary service; at least six months, if the decision is reached by December 15 of the second year (or after nine months but prior to eighteen months) of probationary service; at least one year, if the decision is reached after eighteen months of probationary service or if the faculty member has tenure. This provision for terminal notice or salary need not apply in the event that there has been a finding that the conduct which justified dismissal involved moral turpitude. On the recommendation of the faculty hearing committee or the president, the governing board, in determining what, if any, payments will be made beyond the effective date of dismissal, may take into account the length and quality of service of the faculty member.

9. ACADEMIC FREEDOM AND PROTECTION AGAINST DISCRIMINATION

(a) All members of the faculty, whether tenured or not, are entitled to academic freedom as set forth in the 1940 *Statement of Principles on Academic Freedom and Tenure*, formulated by the Association of American Colleges and the American Association of University Professors.

(b) All members of the faculty, whether tenured or not, are entitled to protection against illegal or unconstitutional discrimination by the institution, or discrimination on a basis not demonstrably related to the faculty member's professional performance, including but not limited to race, sex, religion, national origin, age, physical handicap, marital status, or sexual or affectional preference.

10. COMPLAINTS OF VIOLATION OF ACADEMIC FREEDOM OR OF DISCRIMINATION IN NONREAPPOINTMENT

If a faculty member on probationary or other nontenured appointment alleges that a decision against reappointment was based significantly on considerations violative of (1) academic freedom or (2) governing policies on making appointments without prejudice with respect to race, sex, religion, national origin, age, physical handicap, marital status, or sexual or affectional preference, the allegation will be given preliminary consideration by the [insert name of committee], which will seek to settle the matter by informal methods. The allegation will be accompanied by a statement that the faculty member agrees to the presentation, for the consideration of the faculty committees, of such reasons and evidence as the institution may allege in support of its decision. If the difficulty is unresolved at this stage, and if the committee so recommends, the matter will be heard in the manner set forth in Regulations 5 and 6, except that the faculty member making the complaint is responsible for stating the grounds upon which the allegations are based, and the burden of proof will rest upon the faculty member. If the faculty member succeeds in establishing a *prima facie* case, it is incumbent upon those who made the decision against reappointment to come forward with evidence in support of their decision. Statistical evidence of improper discrimination may be used in establishing a *prima facie* case.

11. ADMINISTRATIVE PERSONNEL

The foregoing regulations apply to administrative personnel who hold academic rank, but only in their capacity as faculty members. Administrators who allege that a consideration violative of academic freedom, or of governing policies against improper discrimination as stated in Regulation 10, significantly contributed to a decision to terminate their appointment to an administrative post, or not to reappoint them, are entitled to the procedures set forth in Regulation 10.

12. POLITICAL ACTIVITIES OF FACULTY MEMBERS

Faculty members, as citizens, are free to engage in political activities. Where necessary, leaves of absence may be given for the duration of an election campaign or a term of office, on timely application, and for a reasonable period of time. The terms of such leave of absence will be set forth in writing, and the leave will not affect unfavorably the tenure status of a faculty member, except that time spent on such leave will not count as probationary service unless otherwise agreed to.[10]

[NOTE: Regulations 13, 14, and 15 are suggested in tentative form, and will require adaptation to the specific structure and operations of the institution; the provisions as recommended here are intended only to indicate the nature of the provisions to be included, and not to offer specific detail.]

13. GRADUATE STUDENT ACADEMIC STAFF

(a) The terms and conditions of every appointment to a graduate or teaching assistantship will be stated in writing, and a copy of the appointment document will be supplied to the graduate or teaching assistant.
(b) In no case will a graduate or teaching assistant be dismissed without having been provided with a statement of reasons and an opportunity to be heard before a duly constituted committee. (A dismissal is a termination before the end of the period of appointment.)
(c) A graduate or teaching assistant who establishes a *prima facie* case to the satisfaction of a duly constituted committee that a decision against reappointment was based significantly on considerations violative of academic freedom, or of governing policies against improper discrimination as stated in Regulation 10, will be given a statement of reasons by those responsible for the nonreappointment and an opportunity to be heard by the committee.
(d) Graduate or teaching assistants will have access to the faculty grievance committee, as provided in Regulation 15.

14. OTHER ACADEMIC STAFF

(a) In no case will a member of the academic staff[11] who is not otherwise protected by the preceding regulations which relate to dismissal proceedings be dismissed without having been provided with a statement of reasons and an opportunity to be heard before a duly constituted committee. (A dismissal is a termination before the end of the period of appointment.)
(b) With respect to the nonreappointment of a member of such academic staff who establishes a *prima facie* case to the satisfaction of a duly constituted committee that a consideration violative of academic freedom, or of governing policies against improper discrimination as stated in Regulation 10, significantly contributed to the nonreappointment, the academic staff member will be given a statement of reasons by those responsible for the nonreappointment and an opportunity to be heard by the committee.

[10]See "Statement on Professors and Political Activity," *AAUP Bulletin* 55 (1969): 388–89.
[11]Each institution should define with particularity who are members of the academic staff.

15. GRIEVANCE PROCEDURE

(a) If any faculty member alleges cause for grievance in any matter not covered by the procedures described in the foregoing regulations, the faculty member may petition the elected
faculty grievance committee [here name the committee] for redress. The petition will set
forth in detail the nature of the grievance and will state against whom the grievance is
directed. It will contain any factual or other data which the petitioner deems pertinent
to the case. Statistical evidence of improper discrimination, including discrimination in
salary,[11] may be used in establishing a *prima facie* case. The committee will decide whether
or not the facts merit a detailed investigation; if the faculty member succeeds in establishing a *prima facie* case, it is incumbent upon those who made the decision to come forward
with evidence in support of their decision. Submission of a petition will not automatically
entail investigation or detailed consideration thereof. The committee may seek to bring
about a settlement of the issue satisfactory to the parties. If in the opinion of the committee such a settlement is not possible or is not appropriate, the committee will report its
findings and recommendations to the petitioner and to the appropriate administrative officer and faculty body, and the petitioner will, upon request, be provided an opportunity
to present the grievance to them. The grievance committee will consist of three [or some
other number] elected members of the faculty. No officer of administration will serve on
the committee.

NOTE ON IMPLEMENTATION

The Recommended Institutional Regulations here presented will require for their implementation a number of structural arrangements and agencies. For example, the Regulations will need
support by:
(a) channels of communication among all the involved components of the institution, and between them and a concerned faculty member.
(b) definitions of corporate and individual faculty status within the college or university government, and of the role of the faculty in decisions relating to academic freedom and tenure.
(c) appropriate procedures for the creation and operation of faculty committees, with particular regard to the principles of faculty authority and responsibility.

The forms which these supporting elements assume will of course vary from one institution
to another. Consequently, no detailed description of the elements is attempted in these Recommended Institutional Regulations. With respect to the principles involved, guidance will be found
in the 1966 *Statement on Government of Colleges and Universities,* jointly formulated by the American Council on Education, the Association of Governing Boards of Universities and Colleges,
and the American Association of University Professors.

[12]See Elizabeth L. Scott, *Higher Education Salary Evaluation Kit* (Washington, D.C.: American Association
of University Professors, 1977).

Standards for Notice of Nonreappointment

The following statement was adopted by the Council of the American Association of University Professors in October 1963 and endorsed by the Fiftieth Annual Meeting in 1964 as Association policy. In 1989 and 1990, the appropriate Association bodies adopted several changes in language in order to remove gender-specific references from the original text.

B ecause a probationary appointment, even though for a fixed or stated term, carries an expectation of renewal, the faculty member should be explicitly informed of a decision not to renew an appointment, in order that the faculty member may seek a position at another college or university. Such notice should be given at an early date, since a failure to secure another position for the ensuing academic year will deny the faculty member the opportunity to continue in the profession. The purpose of this statement is to set forth in detail, for the use of the academic profession, those standards for notice of nonreappointment which the Association over a period of years has actively supported and which are expressed as a general principle in the 1940 *Statement of Principles on Academic Freedom and Tenure.*

THE STANDARDS FOR NOTICE

Notice of nonreappointment, or of intention not to recommend reappointment to the governing board, should be given in writing in accordance with the following standards:

(1) *Not later than March 1 of the first academic year of service*, if the appointment expires at the end of that year; or, if a one-year appointment terminates during an academic year, at least three months in advance of its termination.

(2) *Not later than December 15 of the second academic year of service*, if the appointment expires at the end of that year; or, if an initial two-year appointment terminates during an academic year, at least six months in advance of its termination.

(3) At least twelve months before the expiration of an appointment after two or more years in the institution.

Statement on Professors and Political Activity

The statement which follows was prepared by a subcommittee of Committee A on Academic Freedom and Tenure and approved by Committee A. It was adopted by the Council of the American Association of University Professors in May 1969, and endorsed by the Fifty-fifth Annual Meeting as Association policy. It was endorsed in 1970 by the Association of American Colleges. The governing bodies of the associations, meeting respectively in November 1989 and January 1990, eliminated five introductory paragraphs that were no longer applicable and adopted several changes in language in order to remove gender-specific references from the original text.

INTRODUCTION

The institutional regulations of many colleges and universities govern the participation of professors in political activity and public office holding. These regulations vary from absolute prohibitions against holding public office, campaigning for public office, or participating in the management of political campaigns, to requirements that professors engaging in such political activities merely inform administrative authorities in the college or university of their activities.

In view of the range and variety of institutional and legislative restrictions on political activities of professors, the American Association of University Professors and the Association of American Colleges believe there is a need for a definition of rights and obligations in this area. The following statement is offered as a guide to practice. It is hoped that colleges and universities will formulate and publish regulations consistent with these principles.

STATEMENT

1. College and university faculty members are citizens, and, like other citizens, should be free to engage in political activities so far as they are able to do so consistently with their obligations as teachers and scholars.
2. Many kinds of political activity (e.g., holding part-time office in a political party, seeking election to any office under circumstances that do not require extensive campaigning, or serving by appointment or election in a part-time political office) are consistent with effective service as members of a faculty. Other kinds of political activity (e.g., intensive campaigning for elective office, serving in a state legislature, or serving a limited term in a full-time position) will often require that professors seek a leave of absence from their college or university.
3. In recognition of the legitimacy and social importance of political activity by professors, universities and colleges should provide institutional arrangements to permit it, similar to those applicable to other public or private extramural service. Such arrangements may include the reduction of the faculty member's workload or a leave of absence for the duration of an election campaign or a term of office, accompanied by equitable adjustment of compensation when necessary.
4. Faculty members seeking leaves should recognize that they have a primary obligation to their institution and to their growth as educators and scholars; they should be mindful of

the problem which a leave of absence can create for their administration, their colleagues, and their students; and they should not abuse the privilege by too frequent or too late application or too extended a leave. If adjustments in their favor are made, such as reduction of workload, they should expect the adjustments to be limited to a reasonable period.

5. A leave of absence incident to political activity should come under the institution's normal rules and regulations for leaves of absence. Such a leave should not affect unfavorably the tenure status of a faculty member, except that time spent on such leave from academic duties need not count as probationary service. The terms of a leave and its effect on the professor's status should be set forth in writing.

Academic Freedom and Artistic Expression

---

*The statement which follows was adopted by the participants in the 1990 Wolf Trap Confer-
ence on Academic Freedom and Artistic Expression, sponsored by the American Association of
University Professors, the American Council on Education, the Association of Governing
Boards of Universities and Colleges, and the Wolf Trap Foundation. The statement was endorsed by AAUP's Committee A on Academic Freedom and Tenure and by its Council at their
meetings in June 1990.*

Attempts to curtail artistic presentations at academic institutions on grounds that the works
are offensive to some members of the campus community and of the general public occur
with disturbing frequency. Those who support restrictions argue that works presented
to the public rather than in the classroom or in other entirely intramural settings should conform to their view of the prevailing community standard rather than to standards of academic
freedom. We believe that, "essential as freedom is for the relation and judgment of facts, it is
even more indispensable to the imagination."[1] In our judgment academic freedom in the creation and presentation of works in the visual and the performing arts, by ensuring greater opportunity for imaginative exploration and expression, best serves the public and the academy.
   The following proposed policies are designed to assist academic institutions to respond to the
issues that may arise from the presentation of artistic works to the public and to do so in a manner which preserves academic freedom:

   1) *Academic Freedom in Artistic Expression.* Faculty members and students engaged in the creation and presentation of works of the visual and the performing arts are as much engaged
   in pursuing the mission of the college or university as are those who write, teach, and study
   in other academic disciplines. Works of the visual and the performing arts are important
   both in their own right and because they can enhance our understanding of social institutions and the human condition. Artistic expression in the classroom, the studio, and the
   workshop therefore merits the same assurance of academic freedom that is accorded to other
   scholarly and teaching activities. Since faculty and student artistic presentations to the public
   are integral to their teaching, learning, and scholarship, these presentations merit no less
   protection. Educational and artistic criteria should be used by all who participate in the selection and presentation of artistic works. Reasonable content-neutral regulation of the "time,
   place, and manner" of presentations should be developed and maintained. Academic institutions are obliged to ensure that regulations and procedures do not impair freedom of
   expression or discourage creativity by subjecting artistic work to tests of propriety or ideology.

   2) *Accountability.* Artistic performances and exhibitions in academic institutions encourage artistic creativity, expression, learning, and appreciation. The institutions do not thereby endorse the specific artistic presentations, nor do the presentations necessarily represent the
   institution. This principle of institutional neutrality does not relieve institutions of general
   responsibility for maintaining professional and educational standards, but it does mean that
   institutions are not responsible for the views or the attitudes expressed in specific artistic

---

[1]Helen C. White, "Our Most Urgent Professional Task," *AAUP Bulletin* 45 (March 1959): 282.

works any more than they would be for the content of other instruction, scholarly publication, or invited speeches. Correspondingly, those who present artistic work should not represent themselves or their work as speaking for the institution and should otherwise fulfill their educational and professional responsibilities.

3) *The Audience.* When academic institutions offer exhibitions or performances to the public, they should ensure that the rights of the presenters and of the audience are not impaired by a "heckler's veto" from those who may be offended by the presentation. Academic institutions should ensure that those who choose to view an exhibition or attend a performance may do so without interference. Mere presentation in a public place does not create a "captive audience." Institutions may reasonably designate specific places as generally available or unavailable for exhibitions or performances.

4) *Public Funding.* Public funding for artistic presentations and for academic institutions does not diminish (and indeed may heighten) the responsibility of the university community to ensure academic freedom and of the public to respect the integrity of academic institutions. Government imposition on artistic expression of a test of propriety, ideology, or religion is an act of censorship which impermissibly denies the academic freedom to explore, to teach, and to learn.

On the Imposition of
Tenure Quotas

The statement which follows was approved by the Association's Committee A on Academic Freedom and Tenure and adopted by the Council of the American Association of University Professors in October 1973.

Many institutions of higher education have had to consider ways of accommodating the number and composition of their faculty to a static or declining financial situation. The Association has developed criteria applicable where a reduction in faculty positions is contemplated because of financial exigency or discontinuance of a program.[1] This statement will concern itself with institutional policies designed to shape the overall composition of the faculty by limiting the number of tenured positions, and especially with those policies which establish a fixed maximum percentage of faculty who may possess tenure at a given time.[2]

The Association, while recognizing the concerns that motivate such quotas, opposes them. They are an unwise solution to the problem they purport to solve, and can have grave consequences for the institutions that adopt them. Moreover, they are not compelled, for there are other more nearly satisfactory alternatives available.

Recognizing that tenure best protects academic freedom, but that it is usually undesirable to afford tenure automatically upon an individual's joining a faculty, the American Association of University Professors has supported the employment of a stated maximum probationary period, of sufficient but not excessive length, during which the academic qualifications and performance of newer faculty members can be evaluated in terms of institutional standards and expectations. Indeed, it is principally to provide each institution with a reasonable opportunity of assessing the skills of probationary appointees in terms of its tenure standards (and the availability of others whom it may also desire to consider for tenured appointment) that this Association has not favored policies of automatic tenure. However, to continue the service of faculty members beyond the maximum probationary period, while withholding tenure, presents an unwarranted hazard to their academic freedom.

Accordingly, institutions may properly set high standards for tenure, but they subvert the functions of tenure standards if they provide that, no matter how clearly nontenured faculty members meet any stated academic standard (and no matter how well they compare with the tenured faculty and all others whom the institution is able to attract to that faculty), the system is such as to require their termination from the very positions in which they have served with

---

[1]See Regulations 4(c) and 4(d) of Committee A's "Recommended Institutional Regulations on Academic Freedom and Tenure" (*Academe* 69 [January–February 1983]: 16a–17a). See also the Association's statement on "The Role of the Faculty in Budgetary and Salary Matters" (*AAUP Bulletin* 62 [1976]: 379–81) and "On Institutional Policies Resulting from Financial Exigency: Some Operating Guidelines" (*ibid.* 60 [1974]: 267–68).

[2]The report and recommendations of the Commission on Academic Tenure in Higher Education, published in 1973, called for "policies relating to the proportion of tenured and nontenured faculty that will be compatible with the composition of [the institution's] present staff, its resources, and its future objectives." See *Faculty Tenure* (San Francisco: Jossey-Bass, 1973), pp. 45–51, and particularly the commission's recommendation on pages 50 and 51.

unqualified distinction. Holding faculty members in nontenured service, and then releasing them because a numerical limit on tenured positions prohibits their retention, has the effect of nullifying probation. All full-time appointments, excepting only special appointments of specified brief duration and reappointments of retired faculty members on special conditions, should be either probationary relating to continuous tenure or with continuous tenure.[3] To make appointments which are destined to lead to nonretention because of a fixed numerical quota of tenured positions, obviating any realistic opportunity for the affected individuals to be evaluated for tenure on their academic record, is to depart from a basic feature of the system of tenure and thus to weaken the protections of academic freedom.

A variation to nonretention because of a tenure quota, one which Committee A finds wholly inimical to the principles of academic freedom which tenure serves, is the policy adopted at a few institutions of withholding tenure from admittedly qualified candidates who have completed the maximum probationary period but retaining them in a kind of holding pattern, perpetually more vulnerable than their tenured colleagues to termination, unless and until the quota eases for them and they too are granted tenure. Assuming they have fully earned an entitlement to tenure, there can be no justification for continuing them in a less favorable and more vulnerable status than their tenured colleagues.

Committee A, accordingly, opposes the adoption of tenure quotas for the following reasons:
(a) if combined with the possibility of additional term contracts beyond the period of maximum probationary service plainly adequate to determine the individual's entitlement to tenure, the system indefensibly extends conditions of jeopardy to academic freedom;
(b) probation with automatic termination is not probation; those whom quotas affect by automatically excluding them from consideration for tenure essentially are reduced to a terminal class of contract workers rendered incapable of full and equal faculty membership irrespective of the nature of the service they have given and irrespective of the professional excellence of that service;
(c) in designating a portion of the probationary regular faculty as ineligible to continue, in order to cope with needs of staff flexibility and financial constraints, a quota system is a crude and unjust substitute for more equitable methods of academic planning.

Committee A, in registering its concern over the fixing of a maximum numerical percentage of tenured faculty, does not suggest that an institution should be unconcerned with appointment policies which will permit it to bring new members into its faculty with some regularity. A sound academic program needs elements not only of continuity but also of flexibility, which is served by the continuing opportunity to recruit new persons and to pursue new academic emphases. It is desirable for a faculty to include those recently arrived from the seminars of our graduate schools as well as those who are well established as scholars and teachers.

Such considerations of flexibility are often adduced in support of tenure quotas. But this misses two central points. First, the system of tenure does not exist as subordinate to convenience and flexibility. The protection of academic freedom must take precedence over the claimed advantages of increased flexibility.

Second, imposing a numerical limit on the percentage of tenured faculty disregards a range of other ways to attain a desired mix of senior and junior faculty. Indeed, it imposes an inequitable burden on a vulnerable portion of the faculty in a facile response to issues of academic staffing that should reflect far more comprehensive planning. Establishing fixed quotas may deprive the profession of a large part of the generation of scholars and teachers who currently populate the nontenured positions at our colleges and universities. It would be preferable by far to employ a variety of other measures—some affecting tenured faculty, others affecting probationary and nontenured faculty, and still others affecting prospective faculty members—to ensure that the necessary burdens of financial stringency and lack of growth are shared to some extent by all academic generations.

[3]See "Recommended Institutional Regulations on Academic Freedom and Tenure," Regulation 1(b).

While opposing the imposition of tenure quotas, Committee A recognizes that the general proportion of a faculty on tenure can have an important long-range bearing on the nature and quality of an institution of higher education. Given a situation in which there is small prospect for significant growth in the total size of the faculty, considerations which merit attention include:

A. The desired distribution of tenured and nontenured faculty should be viewed as a long-term goal rather than a short-term solution. The ratio of tenured to nontenured faculty is itself the dynamic consequence of a complex of academic decisions and developments, each of which can be reconsidered. These include: (1) the rate of growth of the institution and its faculty; (2) the fraction of those appointed initially to tenured or probationary positions; (3) the use of visiting faculty members; (4) the use of graduate assistants; (5) the average length of the probationary period of nontenured faculty members who ultimately achieve tenure; (6) the fraction of nontenured faculty members who ultimately achieve tenure; (7) the institutional policy on retirement; and (8) the age distribution of the total faculty.

B. A satisfactory long-range plan may well imply that, along the way, the proportion of the faculty on tenure will at first increase and then, as the force of the plan takes effect, decrease. Just as the end of growth in the size of the faculty leads to a gradual increase in the proportion of those tenured, so the gradual aging of the present faculty will ultimately lead to a tendency for the proportion to decline. Most changes in academic personnel policies require some lag in time before full implementation and impact, and there is nothing disastrous in a temporary bulge in the percentage of faculty members on tenure. On the other hand, long-range injury to an institution may result from rigid and hasty application of any single presumed remedy, such as the imposition of a fixed quota.

C. It should be recognized that, in the short run, reducing the proportion of a faculty on tenure produces very little benefit by way of flexibility. It is only over a period of several years that a change in the proportion acquires pertinency. If an institution finds itself, at the beginning of development of a long-range plan, at or near a preferred distribution which it wishes generally to maintain, it may well be sensible to choose consciously to exceed the desired distribution temporarily while the steps necessary to return to that distribution take effect.

D. Equity and institutional morale demand that all or almost all of the burden of satisfying the desired tenure ratio should not be placed upon the probationary faculty. Attractive accelerated retirement opportunities for senior tenured faculty present one possible alternative. Additionally, consideration may be given to planning carefully the proportion of teaching and research done by full-time and part-time tenured and probationary faculty, teaching assistants, and temporary appointees.

Foreclosing promotion to a tenured position because of a numerical quota is unacceptable. Stricter standards for the awarding of tenure can be developed over the years, with a consequent decrease in the probability of achieving tenure. But it is essential to distinguish a deliberate change in standards, retaining a positive probability of an individual's achieving tenure pursuant to well-defined criteria and adequate procedures for evaluation and review, from a situation in which the granting of tenure, for reasons unrelated to the individual's merits, is never a realistic possibility.

Senior Appointments with Reduced Loads

The statement which follows was approved for publication, by Committee W on the Status of Women in April 1987 and by Committee A on Academic Freedom and Tenure in June 1987, for the information of the profession.

In its 1980 report *On the Status of Part-Time Faculty*, Committee A noted that the 1940 *Statement of Principles on Academic Freedom and Tenure* "refers, with respect to tenure, only to those appointed to full-time service." The concept rested on a view of part-time service as occasional, adjunct, and cost-effective in terms of flexibility; it assumed no ongoing institutional commitment; and it assumed that part-timers were properly relieved of responsibility for the institution's academic program.

Committee A's 1980 report reflected a significant change in perceptions of the nature of part-time service. Citing the 1973 recommendation of the Commission on Academic Tenure in Higher Education, the report agreed that institutions should "consider modifying their tenure arrangements in order to permit part-time faculty service under appropriate conditions to be credited toward the award of tenure, and to permit tenure positions to be held by faculty members who for family or other appropriate reasons cannot serve on a full-time basis." While Committee A recognized that many part-timers are not potential candidates for tenure, it recommended that colleges and universities "consider creating a class of regular part-time faculty members, consisting of individuals who, as their professional career, share the teaching, research, and administrative duties customary for faculty at their institution, but who for whatever reason do so less than full-time." This class of part-timers, the report concluded, "should have the opportunity to achieve tenure and the rights it confers."

Additional benefit would be derived from policies and practices that open senior academic appointments to persons with reduced loads and salaries without loss of status.

In the light of Committee A's recommendation, a senior appointee might choose, for whatever reason, to reduce proportionately his or her overall duties at the institution. If the faculty member were tenured, there would be no loss of the protections of due process and the other entitlements that accrue with tenure;[1] if the faculty member were nontenured, the policy might permit continuance with an "opportunity to achieve tenure and the rights it confers."

These appointments would not normally be made available if the individual were seeking reduction of the academic commitment in order to accept a teaching position elsewhere. Criteria for professional advancement, including promotion in rank, should be the same for all faculty appointees, whether they serve full-time or with reduced loads. Where there is mutual agreement among the faculty member, the department, and the college or university administration, opportunity should exist for a faculty member to move from a full to a reduced load and back to full-time status, depending on the needs of the individual and the institution.

---

[1] Where the action to reduce a full-time tenured faculty member to part-time status is mandated by a declared financial exigency or discontinuance of program, AAUP policy calls for the preservation of the protections of tenure and for continuance of salary on a *pro rata* basis. (See Committee A report on "Academic Freedom and Tenure: Eastern Oregon State College," *Academe* 68 [May–June 1982]: 1a–8a, for further discussion of this issue.)

These modified appointments would help meet the special needs of individual faculty members, especially those with child-rearing and other personal responsibilities, as well as those seeking a reduced workload as a step toward retirement. A more flexible policy for senior appointments (whether tenured or nontenured) would increase the opportunities available both to individuals and to institutions with respect to faculty appointments.

Arbitration in Cases of Dismissal
A Report of a Joint Subcommittee of Committees A and N

The report which follows was approved for publication by the Council of the American Association of University Professors in June 1983.

In 1973, Committee A on Academic Freedom and Tenure and Committee N on Representation of Economic and Professional Interests approved publication in the *AAUP Bulletin* of a report which was addressed to the topic "Arbitration of Faculty Grievances."[1] That report, prepared by a joint subcommittee, was viewed by the committees as a first statement on the relationship of arbitration of faculty grievances to established Association policies. The present report amplifies on the development of arbitral practices in higher education, with particular emphasis on the question of arbitration of dismissal cases.[2] Consistent with the Association's longstanding obligations to the profession to define sound academic practice, this report was prepared after analysis of collective bargaining agreements reached by agents, AAUP and otherwise, and of the relationship of contractual provisions for dismissal to the 1940 *Statement of Principles on Academic Freedom and Tenure*, the 1958 *Statement on Procedural Standards in Faculty Dismissal Proceedings*, and the 1966 *Statement on Government of Colleges and Universities*. It should be added parenthetically that arbitration of faculty status disputes is not limited to institutions with collective bargaining agreements. Members of the subcommittee were aware of one large public system and one large private university which do not have collective bargaining, but which do have faculty regulations that provide for arbitration of certain faculty status matters.

As was noted in the 1973 report, the *Statement on Government of Colleges and Universities*, drafted jointly by the Association, the American Council on Education, and the Association of Governing Boards of Universities and Colleges, gives to the faculty primary responsibility for making decisions on faculty status and related matters. The *Statement on Government* asserts, "The governing board and president should, on questions of faculty status, as in other matters where the faculty has primary responsibility, concur with the faculty judgment except in rare instances and for compelling reasons which should be stated in detail."

Any discussion of Association policy on dismissals should, of course, begin with the provisions of the 1940 *Statement of Principles on Academic Freedom and Tenure* and the 1958 *Statement on Procedural Standards in Faculty Dismissal Proceedings*. Both documents are joint policies of the Association and the Association of American Colleges. The "Academic Tenure" section of the 1940 *Statement* includes a basic outline of the procedural steps necessary for review of the termination for cause of a teacher previous to the expiration of a term appointment. The 1958 *Statement on Procedural Standards in Faculty Dismissal Proceedings* supplements the 1940 *Statement* by describing the academic due process that should be observed in dismissal proceedings. The Association has also provided a fuller codification of appropriate dismissal procedures in Regulations 5 and 6 of its *Recommended Institutional Regulations on Academic Freedom and Tenure*.

[1] *AAUP Bulletin* 59 (1973): 163–67.
[2] The comments on arbitration of dismissal cases are also applicable to those instances in which an administration seeks not to dismiss, but to impose a severe sanction; *cf.* the Association's "Recommended Institutional Regulations on Academic Freedom and Tenure," Regulation 7(a) (*Academe* 69 [January–February 1983]: 15a–20a).

COLLECTIVE BARGAINING MODIFICATION

Collective bargaining normally results in a formally negotiated contract governing terms and conditions of employment; the provisions of the collective agreement define the legal rights and duties of faculty, administrators, and trustees. Customarily, the collective agreement authorizes a neutral third party, an arbitrator, to resolve disputes which arise under it. In contrast to most litigation, negotiated arbitration clauses afford the administration and the faculty opportunity to prescribe the procedures and standards which apply and, most important, jointly to select the decision maker.

It is appropriate to restate here the four factors which the 1973 subcommittee noted as essential for the effective use of arbitration:

1. sound internal procedures preliminary to arbitration which enjoy the confidence of both faculty and administration;
2. careful definition of both arbitral subjects and standards to be applied by arbitration;
3. the selection of arbitrators knowledgeable in the ways of the academic world, aware of the institutional implications of their decisions, and, of course, sensitive to the meaning and critical value of academic freedom; and
4. the assurance that the hearing will include evidence relating to the standards and expectations of the teaching profession in higher education and that appropriate weight will be given to such evidence.

This subcommittee concludes that in cases of dismissal the faculty member may properly be given the right, following a proceeding in accordance with the 1958 *Statement on Procedural Standards in Faculty Dismissal Proceedings* and the *Recommended Institutional Regulations*, to appeal a negative decision to an arbitrator. The subcommittee believes that the 1958 *Statement* provides the most appropriate model for faculty dismissal proceedings. However, where alternatives are implemented, it urges that they should at least make provision for meaningful faculty participation in the dismissal process and for compliance with the requirements of academic due process in the formal dismissal hearing.

ESSENTIAL PRELIMINARY FACULTY PARTICIPATION

Before any formal procedures are invoked, the subcommittee believes that the essential faculty procedures preliminary to any contemplated dismissal, already set forth in Association policy statements,[3] should be followed. The subcommittee is particularly disturbed by contractual dismissal procedures which do not provide in any way for formal faculty participation in a mediative effort prior to the formulation of dismissal charges. It is the subcommittee's opinion that such participation is necessary both to resolve disputes short of formal proceedings and to advise the administration on the wisdom of further pursuit of a particular matter.

In the event that an administration, after receiving faculty advice, chooses to formulate charges for dismissal of a tenured member of an institution's faculty or a nontenured faculty member during the term of appointment, a hearing of the charges should be held, whether or not the faculty member exercises the right to participate in the hearing. A dismissal is not simply a grievance which may not be pursued. A dismissal is a sanction of the highest order requiring a demonstration of cause regardless of the faculty member's individual action or inaction in contesting the charge.

ARBITRATION FOLLOWING A FACULTY HEARING

It is common practice with the profession that, following a hearing before a faculty committee, the hearing committee presents a report to the president who, in turn, either accepts the

[3]See "Statement on Procedural Standards in Faculty Dismissal Proceedings," *Academe* 76 (May–June 1990), Section 1; and "Recommended Institutional Regulations on Academic Freedom and Tenure," *Academe* 69 (January–February 1983), Regulation 5(c)(1).

report or returns it to the committee with reasons for its rejection prior to transmittal of the report to the governing board. The governing board, in turn, has traditionally made the final decision after study of the recommendations presented to it. In the event that the board disagrees with the faculty committee's recommendations, the board should remand the matter to the committee and provide an opportunity for reconsideration. This subcommittee recommends that, after the board's ruling, a faculty member who has pursued these traditional procedures should be given the right to proceed to arbitration. If the collective bargaining agreement provides for arbitration of faculty status disputes, it would be anomalous to deny the right to arbitrate a dismissal, while lesser matters dealing with faculty status may be arbitrated. More important, arbitration in this setting is not a substitute for unfettered trustee judgment, but for the courts; thus, it is not a question of whether institutional officers will be subject to external review, but of what forum is best equipped to perform the task.

It is normally the collective bargaining representative's responsibility to control access to arbitration. The subcommittee believes, however, that the issue of dismissal is of such magnitude that an individual against whom dismissal charges have been sustained by the institutional review processes up to and including the institution's board of trustees should have an unfettered right to seek arbitral review. Moreover, the nature of a dismissal charge against an individual is such, with each case standing on its own merits, that arbitration decisions in dismissal cases should not be considered to have created precedent for other arbitrations dealing with dismissals.

Thus, the subcommittee recommends that, in cases where the collective bargaining representative decides not to appeal a dismissal to arbitration, the individual be given the right to seek arbitral review independently. In that event, the individual would be expected to bear those costs of the arbitration normally assumed by the collective bargaining representative.

As the 1973 subcommittee noted, it is of critical importance "...that in the agreement to arbitrate any matter affecting faculty status, rights, and responsibilities, the judgment of the faculty as a professional body properly vested with the primary responsibility for such determinations be afforded a strong presumption in its favor." This subcommittee agrees and accordingly recommends that, particularly on questions of academic fitness and the norms of the profession, the arbitrator should give great weight to the findings and recommendations of the faculty hearing committee.

The subcommittee recommends that the collective bargaining agreement not limit the scope of the issues which may come to an arbitrator in a dismissal case. The arbitration decision should, of course, be based on the record. The subcommittee recommends that the collective bargaining agent have the right to participate in the proceedings in order to inform the arbitrator fully about the standards applicable to the case under review. The recommendation to permit the arbitrator to examine the procedures leading to the dismissal charges, the procedures for review of the charges, and the substance of the record developed in the hearings before the faculty committee as well as the arbitration is based on the expectation that the parties will select an arbitrator sensitive to the standards and practices of the local and national academic communities.

The procedures of the actual arbitration proceeding should be codified in advance and either spelled out in the collective bargaining agreement or, if there is a known policy which would guide the proceeding, referred to in the agreement. One policy often referred to in agreements at private institutions is the Voluntary Labor Arbitration Rules of the American Arbitration Association; agreements at public institutions often cite the arbitration rules of the agency which administers the state's collective bargaining statute.

ALTERNATIVE ARBITRATION PROCEDURES

The above proposal contemplates the addition of arbitration to procedures already required by the 1958 *Statement on Procedural Standards* and the *Recommended Institutional Regulations*. The proposal does no violence to the basic fabric of the 1940 *Statement*, for the basic dismissal decision is arrived at with full due process within the local academic community. Arbitration merely substitutes an expert neutral—jointly selected—for the judiciary in any subsequent contest over whether the decision was procedurally deficient or substantially in error under standards widely recognized in the academic world.

The subcommittee recognizes that, in the interest of expeditious adjudication of dismissal charges, some institutions in collective bargaining have devised alternative dismissal procedures. Such procedures range from direct arbitration of dismissal cases to modifications of the 1958 *Statement* procedures which incorporate arbitration as part of the formal hearing process, thereby obviating the need for an additional arbitration step upon completion of the internal institutional process.

The subcommittee cannot embrace a position that abandons a model of the faculty as a professional body passing judgment upon its members. Thus, it must reject resort to arbitration as a permissible alternative to the 1958 *Statement* procedures unless certain additional requirements are met. Alternative procedures, designed to comply with the spirit of the 1958 *Statement*, would have to be examined on a case-by-case basis. At a minimum, the subcommittee would expect such procedures to comply with the 1958 *Statement on Procedural Standards* in the following respects:

1. There should be specific provision for faculty participation in a mediative effort prior to the formulation of dismissal charges.
2. There should be significant faculty representation on the hearing panel in a formal hearing of any charges.
3. The formal hearing procedures should comply with the requirements of academic due process as outlined in the *Recommended Institutional Regulations*.

SUMMARY

In summary, the subcommittee has concluded that it is permissible to have potential dismissal of a faculty member subject to review of an outside arbitrator who may make a binding decision. Disputes concerning the dismissal of a faculty member from a tenured position or of a nontenured faculty member during the term of appointment require faculty participation in an effort to mediate the dispute and require a formal hearing.

Consistent with the 1958 *Statement on Procedural Standards* and the *Recommended Institutional Regulations*, after presidential and board review we believe arbitral review may be appropriate. Alternative procedures providing for arbitration at an earlier stage may be acceptable, provided they ensure faculty participation in a mediative effort prior to formulation of dismissal charges, significant faculty participation in a hearing of such charges, and adherence in the formal hearing to the procedural requirements of academic due process.

PROFESSIONAL ETHICS

F rom its earliest years, the Association has recognized that the privileges associated with faculty sta- tus create a corresponding obligation to observe suitable professional and ethical standards. In his introductory address to the first meeting of the Association in 1915, President John Dewey proclaimed that one of the Association's priorities would be the development of "professional standards...which will be quite as scrupulous regarding the obligations imposed by freedom as jealous of the freedom itself." A Committee on University Ethics was one of the Association's original standing committees, and Professor Dewey served as its first chair.

The 1940 Statement of Principles on Academic Freedom and Tenure *declares that academic free- dom "carries with it duties correlative with rights." These duties are described in the documents that follow, beginning with the Association's basic* Statement on Professional Ethics. *Other statements provide guidance on particular ethical situations.*

The Association maintains a standing Committee B on Professional Ethics. The Association views ques- tions involving propriety of conduct as best handled within the framework of individual institutions by reference to an appropriate faculty body. While its good offices are available for advice and mediation, the Association's function in the area of ethics is primarily educative: to inform members of the higher educa- tion community about principles of professional ethics and to encourage their observance.

Statement on
Professional Ethics

The statement which follows, a revision of a statement originally adopted in 1966, was approved by Committee B on Professional Ethics, adopted by the Council, and endorsed by the Seventy-third Annual Meeting in June 1987.

INTRODUCTION

From its inception, the American Association of University Professors has recognized that membership in the academic profession carries with it special responsibilities. The Association has consistently affirmed these responsibilities in major policy statements, providing guidance to professors in such matters as their utterances as citizens, the exercise of their responsibilities to students and colleagues, and their conduct when resigning from an institution or when undertaking sponsored research.[1] The *Statement on Professional Ethics* that follows sets forth those general standards that serve as a reminder of the variety of responsibilities assumed by all members of the profession.

In the enforcement of ethical standards, the academic profession differs from those of law and medicine, whose associations act to ensure the integrity of members engaged in private practice. In the academic profession the individual institution of higher learning provides this assurance and so should normally handle questions concerning propriety of conduct within its own framework by reference to a faculty group. The Association supports such local action and stands ready, through the general secretary and Committee B, to counsel with members of the academic community concerning questions of professional ethics and to inquire into complaints when local consideration is impossible or inappropriate. If the alleged offense is deemed sufficiently serious to raise the possibility of adverse action, the procedures should be in accordance with the 1940 *Statement of Principles on Academic Freedom and Tenure*, the 1958 *Statement on Procedural Standards in Faculty Dismissal Proceedings*, or the applicable provisions of the Association's *Recommended Institutional Regulations on Academic Freedom and Tenure*.

THE STATEMENT

I. Professors, guided by a deep conviction of the worth and dignity of the advancement of knowledge, recognize the special responsibilities placed upon them. Their primary responsibility to their subject is to seek and to state the truth as they see it. To this end professors devote their energies to developing and improving their scholarly competence. They accept the obligation to exercise critical self-discipline and judgment in using, extending, and transmitting

---

[1] 1961 *Statement on Recruitment and Resignation of Faculty Members*
1964 *Committee A Statement on Extramural Utterances* (Clarification of sec. 1c of the 1940 *Statement of Principles on Academic Freedom and Tenure*)
1965 *On Preventing Conflicts of Interest in Government-Sponsored Research at Universities*
1966 *Statement on Government of Colleges and Universities*
1967 *Joint Statement on Rights and Freedoms of Students*
1970 *Council Statement on Freedom and Responsibility*
1976 *On Discrimination*
1984 *Sexual Harassment: Suggested Policy and Procedures for Handling Complaints.*

knowledge. They practice intellectual honesty. Although professors may follow subsidiary interests, these interests must never seriously hamper or compromise their freedom of inquiry.

II. As teachers, professors encourage the free pursuit of learning in their students. They hold before them the best scholarly and ethical standards of their discipline. Professors demonstrate respect for students as individuals and adhere to their proper roles as intellectual guides and counselors. Professors make every reasonable effort to foster honest academic conduct and to ensure that their evaluations of students reflect each student's true merit. They respect the confidential nature of the relationship between professor and student. They avoid any exploitation, harassment, or discriminatory treatment of students. They acknowledge significant academic or scholarly assistance from them. They protect their academic freedom.

III. As colleagues, professors have obligations that derive from common membership in the community of scholars. Professors do not discriminate against or harass colleagues. They respect and defend the free inquiry of associates. In the exchange of criticism and ideas professors show due respect for the opinions of others. Professors acknowledge academic debt and strive to be objective in their professional judgment of colleagues. Professors accept their share of faculty responsibilities for the governance of their institution.

IV. As members of an academic institution, professors seek above all to be effective teachers and scholars. Although professors observe the stated regulations of the institution, provided the regulations do not contravene academic freedom, they maintain their right to criticize and seek revision. Professors give due regard to their paramount responsibilities within their institution in determining the amount and character of work done outside it. When considering the interruption or termination of their service, professors recognize the effect of their decision upon the program of the institution and give due notice of their intentions.

V. As members of their community, professors have the rights and obligations of other citizens. Professors measure the urgency of these obligations in the light of their responsibilities to their subject, to their students, to their profession, and to their institution. When they speak or act as private persons they avoid creating the impression of speaking or acting for their college or university. As citizens engaged in a profession that depends upon freedom for its health and integrity, professors have a particular obligation to promote conditions of free inquiry and to further public understanding of academic freedom.

A Statement of the Association's Council: Freedom and Responsibility

The following statement was adopted by the Council of the American Association of University Professors in October 1970. In April 1990, the Council adopted several changes in language that had been approved by Committee B on Professional Ethics in order to remove gender-specific references from the original text.

For more than half a century the American Association of University Professors has acted upon two principles: that colleges and universities serve the common good through learning, teaching, research, and scholarship; and that the fulfillment of this function necessarily rests upon the preservation of the intellectual freedoms of teaching, expression, research, and debate. All components of the academic community have a responsibility to exemplify and support these freedoms in the interests of reasoned inquiry.

The 1940 *Statement of Principles on Academic Freedom and Tenure* asserts the primacy of this responsibility. The *Statement on Professional Ethics* underscores its pertinency to individual faculty members and calls attention to their responsibility, by their own actions, to uphold their colleagues' and their students' freedom of inquiry and to promote public understanding of academic freedom. The *Joint Statement on Rights and Freedoms of Students* emphasizes the shared responsibility of all members of the academic community for the preservation of these freedoms.

Continuing attacks on the integrity of our universities and on the concept of academic freedom itself come from many quarters. These attacks, marked by tactics of intimidation and harassment and by political interference with the autonomy of colleges and universities, provoke harsh responses and counter-responses. Especially in a repressive atmosphere, the faculty's responsibility to defend its freedoms cannot be separated from its responsibility to uphold those freedoms by its own actions.

I.

Membership in the academic community imposes on students, faculty members, administrators, and trustees an obligation to respect the dignity of others, to acknowledge their right to express differing opinions, and to foster and defend intellectual honesty, freedom of inquiry and instruction, and free expression on and off the campus. The expression of dissent and the attempt to produce change, therefore, may not be carried out in ways which injure individuals or damage institutional facilities or disrupt the classes of one's teachers or colleagues. Speakers on campus must not only be protected from violence, but also be given an opportunity to be heard. Those who seek to call attention to grievances must not do so in ways that significantly impede the functions of the institution.

Students are entitled to an atmosphere conducive to learning and to even-handed treatment in all aspects of the teacher-student relationship. Faculty members may not refuse to enroll or teach students on the grounds of their beliefs or the possible uses to which they may put the knowledge to be gained in a course. Students should not be forced by the authority inherent in the instructional role to make particular personal choices as to political action or their own part in society. Evaluation of students and the award of credit must be based on academic performance professionally judged and not on matters irrelevant to that performance, whether personality, race, religion, degree of political activism, or personal beliefs.

It is the mastery teachers have of their subjects and their own scholarship that entitles them to their classrooms and to freedom in the presentation of their subjects. Thus, it is improper for an instructor persistently to intrude material that has no relation to the subject, or to fail to present the subject matter of the course as announced to the students and as approved by the faculty in their collective responsibility for the curriculum.

Because academic freedom has traditionally included the instructor's full freedom as a citizen, most faculty members face no insoluble conflicts between the claims of politics, social action, and conscience, on the one hand, and the claims and expectations of their students, colleagues, and institutions, on the other. If such conflicts become acute, and attention to obligations as a citizen and moral agent precludes an instructor from fulfilling substantial academic obligations, the instructor cannot escape the responsibility of that choice, but should either request a leave of absence or resign his or her academic position.

II.

The Association's concern for sound principles and procedures in the imposition of discipline is reflected in the 1940 *Statement of Principles on Academic Freedom and Tenure*, the 1958 *Statement on Procedural Standards in Faculty Dismissal Proceedings*, the *Recommended Institutional Regulations on Academic Freedom and Tenure*, and the many investigations conducted by the Association into disciplinary actions by colleges and universities.

The question arises whether these customary procedures are sufficient in the current context. We believe that by and large they serve their purposes well, but that consideration should be given to supplementing them in several respects:

First, plans for ensuring compliance with academic norms should be enlarged to emphasize preventive as well as disciplinary action. Toward this end the faculty should take the initiative, working with the administration and other components of the institution, to develop and maintain an atmosphere of freedom, commitment to academic inquiry, and respect for the academic rights of others. The faculty should also join with other members of the academic community in the development of procedures to be used in the event of serious disruption, or the threat of disruption, and should ensure its consultation in major decisions, particularly those related to the calling of external security forces to the campus.

Second, systematic attention should be given to questions related to sanctions other than dismissal, such as warnings and reprimands, in order to provide a more versatile body of academic sanctions.

Third, there is need for the faculty to assume a more positive role as guardian of academic values against unjustified assaults from its own members. The traditional faculty function in disciplinary proceedings has been to ensure academic due process and meaningful faculty participation in the imposition of discipline by the administration. While this function should be maintained, faculties should recognize their stake in promoting adherence to norms essential to the academic enterprise.

Rules designed to meet these needs for faculty self-regulation and flexibility of sanctions should be adopted on each campus in response to local circumstances and to continued experimentation. In all sanctioning efforts, however, it is vital that proceedings be conducted with fairness to the individual, that faculty judgments play a crucial role, and that adverse judgments be founded on demonstrated violations of appropriate norms. The Association will encourage and assist local faculty groups seeking to articulate the substantive principles here outlined or to make improvements in their disciplinary machinery to meet the needs here described. The Association will also consult and work with any responsible group, within or outside the academic community, that seeks to promote understanding of and adherence to basic norms of professional responsibility so long as such efforts are consistent with principles of academic freedom.

Statement on Plagiarism

The statement which follows was approved for publication by the Association's Committee B on Professional Ethics, adopted by the Council in June 1990, and endorsed by the Seventy-sixth Annual Meeting.

T he main practical activity of the American Association of University Professors, since its founding, has concerned restraints upon the right of faculty members to inquire, to teach, to speak, and to publish professionally. Yet throughout its existence, the Association has emphasized the responsibilities of faculty members no less than their rights. Both rights and responsibilities support the common good served by institutions of higher education which, in the words of the 1940 *Statement of Principles on Academic Freedom and Tenure*, "depends upon the free search for truth and its free exposition."

In its *Statement on Professional Ethics*, the Association has stressed the obligation of professors to their subject and to the truth as they see it, as well as the need for them to "exercise critical self-discipline and judgment in using, extending, and transmitting knowledge." Defending free inquiry by their associates and respecting the opinion of others, in the exchange of criticism and ideas, professors must also be rigorously honest in acknowledging their academic debts.

In the light of recent concerns within and outside of the academic profession, it has seemed salutary to restate these general obligations with respect to the offense of plagiarism.

DEFINITION

The offense of plagiarism may seem less self-evident in some circles now than it did formerly. Politicians, business executives, and even university presidents depend on the ideas and literary skills of committees, aides, and speechwriters in the many communications they are called on to make inside and outside their organizations. When ideas are rapidly popularized and spread abroad through the media, when fashion and the quest for publicity are all around us, a concern with protecting the claims of originality may seem to some a quaint survival from the past or even a perverse effort to deter the spread of knowledge.

Nevertheless, within the academic world, where advancing knowledge remains the highest calling, scholars must give full and fair recognition to the contributors to that enterprise, both for the substance and for the formulation of their findings and interpretations. Even within the academic community, however, there are complexities and shades of difference. A writer of textbooks rests on the labors of hundreds of authors of monographs who cannot all be acknowledged; the derivative nature of such work is understood and even, when it is well and skillfully done, applauded. A poet, composer, or painter may "quote" the creation of another artist, deliberately without explanation as a means of deeper exploration of meaning and in the expectation that knowledgeable readers, listeners, or viewers will appreciate the allusion and delight in it. There are even lapses—regrettable but not always avoidable—in which a long-buried memory of something read surfaces as a seemingly new thought.

But none of these situations diminishes the central certainty: taking over the ideas, methods, or written words of another, without acknowledgment and with the intention that they be taken as the work of the deceiver, is plagiarism. It is theft of a special kind, for the true author still retains the original ideas and words, yet they are diminished as that author's property and a fraud is committed upon the audience that believes those ideas and words originated with the deceiver. Plagiarism is not limited to the academic community but has perhaps its most pernicious effect in that setting. It is the antithesis of the honest labor that characterizes true scholarship and without which mutual trust and respect among scholars is impossible.

PRECEPTS

Every professor should be guided by the following:

1. In his or her own work, the professor must scrupulously acknowledge every intellectual debt—for ideas, methods, and expressions—by means appropriate to the form of communication.
2. Any discovery of suspected plagiarism should be brought at once to the attention of the affected parties and, as appropriate, to the profession at large through proper and effective channels—typically through reviews in or communications to relevant scholarly journals. Committee B of the Association stands ready to provide its good offices in resolving questions of plagiarism, either independently or in collaboration with other professional societies.
3. Professors should work to ensure that their universities and professional societies adopt clear guidelines respecting plagiarism, appropriate to the disciplines involved, and should insist that regular procedures be in place to deal with violations of those guidelines. The gravity of a charge of plagiarism, by whomever it is made, must not diminish the diligence exercised in determining whether the accusation is valid. In all cases the most scrupulous procedural fairness must be observed, and penalties must be appropriate to the degree of offense.[1]
4. Scholars must make clear the respective contributions of colleagues on a collaborative project, and professors who have the guidance of students as their responsibility must exercise the greatest care not to appropriate a student's ideas, research, or presentation to the professor's benefit; to do so is to abuse power and trust.
5. In dealing with graduate students, professors must demonstrate by precept and example the necessity of rigorous honesty in the use of sources and of utter respect for the work of others. The same expectations apply to the guidance of undergraduate students, with a special obligation to acquaint students new to the world of higher education with its standards and the means of ensuring intellectual honesty.

CONCLUSION

Any intellectual enterprise—by an individual, a group of collaborators, or a profession—is a mosaic, the pieces of which are put in place by many hands. Viewed from a distance, it should appear a meaningful whole, but the long process of its assemblage must not be discounted or misrepresented. Anyone who is guilty of plagiarism not only harms those most directly affected but also diminishes the authority and credibility of all scholarship and all creative arts, and therefore ultimately harms the interests of the broader society. The danger of plagiarism for teaching, learning, and scholarship is manifest, the need vigorously to maintain standards of professional integrity compelling.

---

[1]On the question of due process for a faculty member who is the subject of disciplinary action because of alleged plagiarism, see Regulations 5 and 7 of the Association's *Recommended Institutional Regulations on Academic Freedom and Tenure* in *Academe* 69 (January–February 1983: 18a–19a).

Statement on Recruitment and Resignation of Faculty Members

The statement printed below was adopted by the Association of American Colleges in January 1961 with the following reservations as set forth in a preamble prepared by that Association's Commission on Academic Freedom and Tenure:

1. No set of principles adopted by the Association can do more than suggest *and recommend a course of action. Consequently, the present statement in no way interferes with institutional sovereignty.*

2. The commission realizes that the diversity of practice and control that exists among institutions of higher learning precludes any set of standards from being universally *applicable to every situation.*

3. The statement is concerned only with minimum *standards and in no way seeks to create a norm for institutions at which "better" practices already are in force.*

4. The commission recognizes the fact that "emergency" situations will arise and will have to be dealt with. However, it urges both administration and faculty to do so in ways that will not go counter to the spirit of cooperation, good faith, and responsibility that the statement is seeking to promote.

5. The commission believes that the spirit embodied in the proposed statement is its most important aspect.

In view of these reservations, the Council of the American Association of University Professors in April 1961 voted approval of the statement without adopting it as a binding obligation. Endorsement of the statement in this form was voted by the Forty-seventh Annual Meeting.

The governing bodies of the Association of American Colleges and the American Association of University Professors, acting respectively in January and April 1990, adopted several changes in language in order to remove gender-specific references from the original text.

Mobility of faculty members among colleges and universities is rightly recognized as desirable in American higher education. Yet the departure of a faculty member always requires changes within the institution and may entail major adjustments on the part of faculty colleagues, the administration, and students in the faculty member's field. Ordinarily a temporary or permanent successor must be found and appointed to either the vacated position or the position of a colleague who is promoted to replace the faculty member. Clear standards of practice in the recruitment and in the resignations of members of existing faculties should contribute to an orderly interchange of personnel that will be in the interest of all.

The standards set forth below are recommended to administrations and faculties, in the belief that they are sound and should be generally followed. They are predicated on the assumption that proper provision has been made by employing institutions for timely notice to probationary faculty members and those on term appointments, with respect to their subsequent status. In addition to observing applicable requirements for notice of termination to probationary faculty members, institutions should make provision for notice to all faculty members, not later than March 15 of each year, of their status the following fall, including rank and (unless unavoidable budgetary procedures beyond the institution forbid) prospective salary.

1. Negotiations looking to the possible appointment for the following fall of persons who are already faculty members at other institutions, in active service or on leave of absence and not

on terminal appointment, should be begun and completed as early as possible in the academic year. It is desirable that, when feasible, the faculty member who has been approached with regard to another position inform the appropriate officers of his or her institution when such negotiations are in progress. The conclusion of a binding agreement for the faculty member to accept an appointment elsewhere should always be followed by prompt notice to the faculty member's current institution.

2. A faculty member should not resign, in order to accept other employment as of the end of the academic year, later than May 15 or 30 days after receiving notification of the terms of continued employment the following year, whichever date occurs later. It is recognized, however, that this obligation will be in effect only if institutions generally observe the time factor set forth in the following paragraph for new offers. It is also recognized that emergencies will occur. In such an emergency the faculty member may ask the appropriate officials of the institution to waive this requirement; but the faculty member should conform to their decision.

3. To permit a faculty member to give due consideration and timely notice to his or her institution in the circumstances defined in paragraph 1 of these standards, an offer of appointment for the following fall at another institution should not be made after May 1. The offer should be a "firm" one, not subject to contingencies.

4. Institutions deprived of the services of faculty members too late in the academic year to permit their replacement by securing the members of other faculties in conformity to these standards, and institutions otherwise prevented from taking timely action to recruit from other faculties, should accept the necessity of making temporary arrangements or obtaining personnel from other sources, including new entrants to the academic profession and faculty personnel who have retired.

5. Except by agreement with their institution, faculty members should not leave or be solicited to leave their positions during an academic year for which they hold an appointment.

On Preventing Conflicts of Interest in Government-Sponsored Research at Universities

The many complex problems that have developed in connection with the extensive sponsored research programs of the federal government have been of concern to the government, the academic community, and private industry. The Association, through its Council, and the American Council on Education, working in cooperation with the president's science advisor and the Federal Council of Science and Technology, in 1965 developed a statement of principles formulating basic standards and guidelines in this problem area.

An underlying premise of the statement is that responsibility for determining standards affecting the academic community rests with that community, and that conflict-of-interest problems are best handled by administration and faculty in cooperative effort. In addition to providing guidelines, the statement seeks to identify and alert administration and faculty to the types of situations that have proved troublesome. Throughout, it seeks to protect the integrity of the objectives and needs of the cooperating institutions and their faculties, as well as of sponsoring agencies.

In April 1990, the Council of the American Association of University Professors adopted several changes in language in order to remove gender-specific references from the original text.

The increasingly necessary and complex relationships among universities, government, and industry call for more intensive attention to standards of procedure and conduct in government-sponsored research. The clarification and application of such standards must be designed to serve the purposes and needs of the projects and the public interest involved in them and to protect the integrity of the cooperating institutions as agencies of higher education.

The government and institutions of higher education, as the contracting parties, have an obligation to see that adequate standards and procedures are developed and applied; to inform one another of their respective requirements; and to ensure that all individuals participating in their respective behalves are informed of and apply the standards and procedures that are so developed.

Consulting relationships between university staff members and industry serve the interests of research and education in the university. Likewise, the transfer of technical knowledge and skill from the university to industry contributes to technological advance. Such relationships are desirable, but certain potential hazards should be recognized.

A. CONFLICT SITUATIONS

1. *Favoring of outside interests.* When a university staff member (administrator, faculty member, professional staff member, or employee) undertaking or engaging in government-sponsored work has a significant financial interest in, or a consulting arrangement with, a private business concern, it is important to avoid actual or apparent conflicts of interest between government-sponsored university research obligations and outside interests and other obligations. Situations in or from which conflicts of interest may arise are the:

a. undertaking or orientation of the staff member's university research to serve the research or other needs of the private firm without disclosure of such undertaking or orientation to the university and to the sponsoring agency;

b. purchase of major equipment, instruments, materials, or other items for university research from the private firm in which the staff member has the interest without disclosure of such interest;

c. transmission to the private firm or other use for personal gain of government-sponsored work products, results, materials, records, or information that are not made generally available (this would not necessarily preclude appropriate licensing arrangements for inventions, or consulting on the basis of government-sponsored research results where there is significant additional work by the staff member independent of the government-sponsored research);

d. use for personal gain or other unauthorized use of privileged information acquired in connection with the staff member's government-sponsored activities (the term "privileged information" includes, but is not limited to, medical, personnel, or security records of individuals; anticipated material requirements or price actions; possible new sites for government operations; and knowledge of forthcoming programs or of selection of contractors or subcontractors in advance of official announcements);

e. negotiation or influence upon the negotiation of contracts relating to the staff member's government-sponsored research between the university and private organizations with which the staff member has consulting or other significant relationships;

f. acceptance of gratuities or special favors from private organizations with which the university does, or may conduct, business in connection with a government-sponsored research project, or extension of gratuities or special favors to employees of the sponsoring government agency, under circumstances which might reasonably be interpreted as an attempt to influence the recipients in the conduct of their duties.

2. *Distribution of effort.* There are competing demands on the energies of faculty members (for example, research, teaching, committee work, outside consulting). The way in which a faculty member divides his or her effort among these various functions does not raise ethical questions unless the government agency supporting the research is misled in its understanding of the amount of intellectual effort the faculty member is actually devoting to the research in question. A system of precise time accounting is incompatible with the inherent character of the work of faculty members, since the various functions they perform are closely interrelated and do not conform to any meaningful division of a standard work week. On the other hand, if the research agreement contemplates that a faculty member will devote a certain fraction of effort to the government-sponsored research, or the faculty member agrees to assume responsibility in relation to such research, a demonstrable relationship between the indicated effort or responsibility and the actual extent of the faculty member's involvement is to be expected. Each university, therefore, should—through joint consultation of administration and faculty—develop procedures to ensure that proposals are responsibly made and complied with.

3. *Consulting for government agencies or their contractors.* When the staff member engaged in government-sponsored research also serves as a consultant to a federal agency, such conduct is subject to the provisions of the Conflict of Interest Statutes (18 U.S.C. 202–209 as amended) and the president's memorandum of May 2, 1963, *Preventing Conflicts of Interest on the Part of Special Government Employees.* When the staff member consults for one or more government contractors, or prospective contractors, in the same technical field as the staff member's research project, care must be taken to avoid giving advice that may be of questionable objectivity because of its possible bearing on the individual's other interests. In undertaking and performing consulting services, the staff member should make full disclosure of such interests to the university and to the contractor insofar as they may appear to relate to the work at the university or for the contractor. Conflict-of-interest problems could arise, for example, in the participation of a staff member of the university in an evaluation for the government agency or its contractor of some technical aspect of the work of another organization with which the staff member has a

consulting or employment relationship or a significant financial interest, or in an evaluation of a competitor to such other organization.

B. UNIVERSITY RESPONSIBILITY

Each university participating in government-sponsored research should make known to the sponsoring government agencies:

1. the steps it is taking to ensure an understanding on the part of the university administration and staff members of the possible conflicts of interest or other problems that may develop in the foregoing types of situations, and
2. the organizational and administrative actions it has taken or is taking to avoid such problems, including:
   a. accounting procedures to be used to ensure that government funds are expended for the purposes for which they have been provided, and that all services which are required in return for these funds are supplied;
   b. procedures that enable it to be aware of the outside professional work of staff members participating in government-sponsored research, if such outside work relates in any way to the government-sponsored research;
   c. the formulation of standards to guide the individual university staff members in governing their conduct in relation to outside interests that might raise questions of conflicts of interest; and
   d. the provision within the university of an informed source of advice and guidance to its staff members for advance consultation on questions they wish to raise concerning the problems that may or do develop as a result of their outside financial or consulting interests, as they relate to their participation in government-sponsored university research. The university may wish to discuss such problems with the contracting officer or other appropriate government official in those cases that appear to raise questions regarding conflicts of interest.

The above process of disclosure and consultation is the obligation assumed by the university when it accepts government funds for research. The process must, of course, be carried out in a manner that does not infringe on the legitimate freedoms and flexibility of action of the university and its staff members that have traditionally characterized a university. It is desirable that standards and procedures of the kind discussed be formulated and administered by members of the university community themselves, through their joint initiative and responsibility, for it is they who are the best judges of the conditions which can most effectively stimulate the search for knowledge and preserve the requirements of academic freedom. Experience indicates that such standards and procedures should be developed and specified by joint administration-faculty action.

Statement on Collective Bargaining

The following statement, a revision of a statement adopted in 1973, was prepared by the Association's Committee N on Representation of Economic and Professional Interests in consultation with the Collective Bargaining Congress. It was approved by Committee N and adopted by the Council in June 1984 and endorsed by the Seventieth Annual Meeting as Association policy.

The basic purposes of the American Association of University Professors are to protect academic freedom, to establish and strengthen institutions of faculty governance, to provide fair procedures for resolving grievances, to promote the economic well-being of faculty and other academic professionals, and to advance the interests of higher education. Collective bargaining is an effective instrument for achieving these objectives.

The presence of institutions of faculty governance does not preclude the need for or usefulness of collective bargaining. On the contrary, collective bargaining can be used to increase the effectiveness of those institutions by extending their areas of competence, defining their authority, and strengthening their voice in areas of shared authority and responsibility. Collective bargaining gives the faculty an effective voice in decisions which vitally affect its members' professional well-being, such as the allocation of financial resources and determination of faculty salaries and benefits.

As a national organization which has historically played a major role in formulating and implementing the principles that govern relationships in academic life, the Association promotes collective bargaining to reinforce the best features of higher education. The principles of academic freedom and tenure, fair procedures, faculty participation in governance, and the primary responsibility of the faculty for determining academic policy will thereby be secured.

For these reasons, the Association supports efforts of local chapters to pursue collective bargaining.

POLICY FOR COLLECTIVE BARGAINING CHAPTERS

A. When a chapter of the Association enters into collective bargaining, it should seek to:
1. protect and promote the professional and economic interests of the faculty as a whole in accordance with the established principles of the Association;
2. maintain and enhance within the institution structures of representative governance which provide full participation by the faculty in accordance with the established principles of the Association;
3. obtain explicit guarantees of academic freedom and tenure in accordance with the principles and stated policies of the Association;
4. create orderly and clearly defined procedures for prompt consideration of problems and grievances of members of the bargaining unit, to which procedures any affected individual or group shall have access.

B. In any agency shop or compulsory dues check-off arrangement, a chapter or other Association agency should incorporate provisions designed to accommodate affirmatively asserted conscientious objection to such an arrangement with any representative.

C. The principle of shared authority and responsibility requires a process of discussion, persuasion, and accommodation within a climate of mutual concern and trust. Where that process and climate exist, there should be no need for any party to resort to devices of economic pressure such as strikes, lockouts, or unilateral changes in terms and conditions of employment by faculty or academic management. Normally, such measures are not desirable for the resolution of conflicts within institutions of higher education.

Therefore, the Association urges faculties and administrations in collective bargaining to seek mutual agreement on methods of dispute resolution, such as mediation, fact-finding, or arbitration. Where such agreement cannot be reached, and where disputes prove themselves resistant to rational methods of discussion, persuasion, and conciliation, the Association recognizes that resort to economic pressure through strikes or other work actions may be a necessary and unavoidable means of dispute resolution.

Participation in a strike or other work action does not by itself constitute grounds for dismissal or for other sanctions against faculty members. Moreover, if action against a faculty member is proposed on this, as on any, ground encompassed by the 1940 *Statement of Principles on Academic Freedom and Tenure*, the proceedings must satisfy the requirements of academic due process supported by the Association. The Association will continue to protect the interests of members of the profession who are singled out for punishment on grounds that are inadequate or unacceptable, or who are not afforded all the protections demanded by the requisites of due process.

Statement on Academic Government for Institutions Engaged in Collective Bargaining

The following statement was approved by the Association's Committee N on Representation of Economic and Professional Interests and Committee T on College and University Government and was adopted by the Council of the American Association of University Professors in June 1988.

The 1966 *Statement on Government of Colleges and Universities* affirms that effective governance of an academic institution requires joint effort based on the community of interest of all parties to the enterprise. In particular, that statement, jointly formulated by AAUP, the American Council on Education, and the Association of Governing Boards of Universities and Colleges, observes that:

> The variety and complexity of the tasks performed by institutions of higher education produce an inescapable interdependence among governing board, administration, faculty, students, and others. The relationship calls for adequate communication among these components and full opportunity for appropriate joint planning and effort.
>
> Joint effort in an academic institution will take a variety of forms appropriate to the kinds of situations encountered.

The various parties engaged in the governance of a college or university bring to higher education differing perspectives based on their differing but complementary roles in the academic effort. Traditional shared governance integrates those differing roles into productive action that will benefit the college or university as a whole. It is in the best interest of all parties to ensure that the institutions of shared governance function as smoothly and effectively as possible. Collective bargaining is one means to that end. As the Association's *Statement on Collective Bargaining* asserts, "collective bargaining can be used to increase the effectiveness of [institutions of faculty governance] by extending their areas of competence, defining their authority, and strengthening their voice in areas of shared authority and responsibility."

Collective bargaining should not replace, but rather should ensure, effective traditional forms of shared governance. The types of governance mechanisms appropriate to a particular college or university are dictated by that institution's needs, traditions, and mission. Since those basic factors are not necessarily affected by the emergence of collective bargaining at a campus, bargaining does not necessarily entail substantive changes in the structure of shared governance appropriate for that institution.

Collective bargaining on a campus usually arises at least in part in response to agencies or forces beyond the scope of institutional governance. When problems in institutional governance do contribute to the emergence of collective bargaining, these problems generally stem less from inadequacy in the structure for shared governance than from a failure in its proper implementation. Bargaining can contribute substantially to the identification, clarification, and correction of such difficulties.

Collective bargaining contributes to problem solving in three primary ways. Formal negotiation can improve communication between the faculty and the administration or governing board.

Such communication is essential if the joint planning and effort urged by the *Statement on Government* is to be productive. Collective bargaining can secure consensus on institutional policies and procedures that delineate faculty and administrative participation in shared governance. Finally, collective bargaining can ensure equitable implementation of established procedures.

Collective bargaining should ensure institutional policies and procedures that provide access for all faculty to participation in shared governance. Employed in this way, collective bargaining complements and supports structures of shared governance consistent with the *Statement on Government*. From a faculty perspective, collective bargaining can strengthen shared governance by specifying and ensuring the faculty role in institutional decision-making. Specification may occur through bargaining of governance clauses that define faculty responsibilities in greater detail; assurance of the faculty's negotiated rights may be provided through a grievance procedure supporting the provisions of the negotiated contract. From an administration perspective, contractual clarification and arbitral review of shared governance can reduce the conflicts occasioned by ill-defined or contested allocation of responsibility and thereby enhance consensus and cooperation in academic governance.

The sharing of authority in the governance of colleges and universities, as the *Statement on Government* asserts, is sound practice for academic institutions to follow. Any process for refining and enforcing proper practice should be viewed by all parties concerned with the welfare of higher education as a welcome addition to academic problem solving. Collective bargaining can be such a process. To be effective, bargaining must allow the parties to confront all aspects of their common problems, without encountering externally imposed barriers to possible solutions. Each party must be free to address matters of legitimate concern, and bargaining should provide an inclusive framework within which the parties will be encouraged to move toward resolution of their differences. For this reason, the scope of bargaining should not be limited in ways that prevent mutual employment of the bargaining process for the clarification, improvement, and assurance of a sound structure of shared governance.

Thus, effective collective bargaining can serve to benefit the institution as a whole as well as its various constituencies. Faculty, administrations, governing boards, and state and federal agencies should cooperate to see that collective bargaining is conducted in good faith. When legislatures, judicial authorities, boards, administrations, or faculty act on the mistaken assumption that collective bargaining is incompatible with collegial governance, they do a grave disservice to the very institutions they seek to serve. The cooperative interaction between faculty and administration that is set forth as a workable ideal in the *Statement on Government* depends on a strong institutional commitment to shared governance. By providing a contractually enforceable foundation to an institution's collegial governance structure, collective bargaining can ensure the effectiveness of that structure and can thereby contribute significantly to the well-being of the institution.

Arbitration of Faculty Grievances
A Report of a Joint Subcommittee
of Committees A and N

The report which follows, prepared by a joint subcommittee of Committee A on Academic Freedom and Tenure and Committee N on Representation of Economic and Professional Interests, was approved for publication by Committees N and A, respectively, in March and April 1973.

I. INTRODUCTION

Collective bargaining by faculties in higher education has been accompanied by the use of arbitration[1] for the resolution of disputes involving questions of contractual application or interpretation which may include matters of faculty status and rights. It should be noted that the use of arbitration does not wholly depend on the existence of a collective bargaining relationship. It may be provided for in institutional regulations, agreed to between an internal faculty governing body and the administration, or utilized on an *ad hoc* basis in a particular case. The enforceability of agreements to arbitrate future disputes, however, is a legal question involving both federal and state law. Since arbitration developed in the industrial context, it must be given the closest scrutiny when applied to the needs of higher education. Accordingly, this joint subcommittee was given the task of providing an initial review of that application.

II. PRELIMINARY CONSIDERATIONS

The Association has been committed, since its founding in 1915, to securing a meaningful role for the faculty in decisions on matters of faculty status, rights, and responsibilities. The *Statement on Government of Colleges and Universities,* drafted jointly with the American Council on Education and the Association of Governing Boards of Universities and Colleges, provides a brief discussion of the bases for this position:

> The primary responsibility of the faculty for such matters is based upon the fact that its judgment is central to general educational policy. Furthermore, scholars in a particular field or activity have the chief competence for judging the work of their colleagues; in such competence it is implicit that responsibility exists for both adverse and favorable judgments. Likewise there is the more general competence of experienced faculty personnel committees having a broader charge. Determinations in these matters should first be by faculty action through established procedures, reviewed by the chief academic officers with the concurrence of the board. The governing board and the president should, on questions of faculty status, as in other matters where the faculty has primary responsibility, concur with the faculty judgment except in rare instances and for compelling reasons which should be stated in detail.

---

[1] Arbitration is a term describing a system for the resolution of disputes whereby the parties consent to submit a controversy to a third party for decision. The decision may be advisory only but is usually agreed to be binding. The parties participate in the selection of the arbitrator and may shape the procedure to be used; costs are usually borne equally between them.

The *Statement* does not suggest a formal device to resolve disputes between faculty and governing board. Indeed, resort to any body outside the institution, such as the courts, for an official resolution of disputes in matters of faculty status, rights, and responsibilities poses a serious challenge to accepted notions of institutional autonomy. Moreover, a survey of current practices, admittedly limited, reveals that arbitration has been used not solely to break impasses between faculty and governing board but to review the soundness of faculty decisions themselves. This suggests an additional problem of the relationships of arbitration to faculty autonomy.

III. THE USE OF ARBITRATION

In many situations, administrators are responsive to faculty recommendations and indeed may welcome them. In such cases the resort to arbitration will probably not be perceived as necessary. In some situations, however, administrators or trustees are unresponsive to Association standards and faculty actions, and final legal authority to resolve matters of faculty status usually lies with the governing board concerned. In such cases, outside impartial review may well be useful. It must also be recognized that in many situations faculty members do not enjoy or exercise a degree of independence adequate to the assurance of protections embodied in Association standards. In this situation also, independent impartial review may play a role. For example, disputes regarding the appropriateness of individual salaries, or the imposition of penalties for alleged violations of institutional regulations, or the termination of academic appointments for reason of financial exigency, or decisions affecting a faculty member's teaching duties or programs of instruction are the sorts of controversies resolution of which may be fostered in varying degrees by arbitration.

It seems clear that where resort to a formal external agency is deemed necessary, arbitration affords some advantages over judicial proceedings. In a court challenge, the procedure and substance are prescribed by federal and state constitutions, statutes, and judicial decisions in whose formulation the profession has almost no role. In contrast, arbitration procedures and substantive rights are largely within the joint power of the administration and the faculty's collective representative to prescribe. Hence the parties to the academic relationship can shape procedures to their special needs, formulate substantive rules embodying the standards of the profession, and select decision-makers with special competence in the field. In addition, arbitration may prove a quicker and less expensive remedy.

Thus, where the faculty does not share in the making of decisions or its voice is not accorded adequate weight, arbitration may have particular utility. However, the finality of arbitral review also has its hazards, especially in the present nascent state of arbitral doctrine, and because of the slight experience of arbitrators in academic settings. Accordingly, arbitration may play a useful role in an academic setting to the extent it can foster rather than impair the sound workings of institutional government.

It is suggested that four factors are essential for the effective use of arbitration: (1) sound internal procedures preliminary to arbitration which enjoy the confidence of both faculty and administration; (2) careful definitions of both arbitral subjects and standards to be applied by the arbitrator; (3) the selection of arbitrators knowledgeable in the ways of the academic world, aware of the institutional implications of their decisions, and, of course, sensitive to the meaning and critical value of academic freedom; and (4) the assurance that the hearing will include evidence relating to the standards and expectations of the teaching profession in higher education and that appropriate weight will be given to such evidence.

1. Preliminary Procedures

Arbitration should be used most discriminatingly. It is not a substitute for proper procedures internal to the institution but should serve only as a final stage of that procedure. The availability of this forum should assist in rendering the earlier procedures more meaningful. Indeed, the submission of an inordinate number of grievances to arbitration may be significantly erosive of healthy faculty-administration relations.

The Association has suggested preliminary procedures for the adjustment of general faculty complaints and grievances.[2] With more detail, the Association has crystallized procedures to be utilized in dismissal proceedings,[3] proposed procedures to be used in hearing allegations of violations of academic freedom in the nonreappointment of nontenured faculty,[4] and, most recently, adopted detailed provisions dealing with decisions on nonreappointment and review therefrom not raising issues of academic freedom.[5]

The subcommittee recognizes that a wide variety of institutional practice exists in American higher education and that the degree to which faculties actually possess the decision-making authority recommended in the foregoing varies accordingly. It may not be possible, then, to propose a single model of arbitration responsive to these varying institutional patterns and the many kinds of issues which could conceivably be presented for an arbitral determination. The subcommittee believes it to be of critical importance, however, that, in the agreement to arbitrate any matter affecting faculty status, rights, and responsibilities, the judgment of the faculty as the professional body properly vested with the primary responsibility for such determinations be accorded a strong presumption in its favor.

2. Arbitral Standards

The definition of the arbitral standards requires the most careful attention. In some instances arbitration has been used to correct only procedural departures, while in others arbitral review of the merits of a decision has been afforded. The latter has proceeded under broad standards such as "just cause" for a particular action or more rigorous ones such as determining whether the questioned decision was "arbitrary and capricious."

A tentative review of arbitral decisions under the varying approaches has revealed widely differing results and in some cases a degree of arbitral unresponsiveness to the underlying academic values. Accordingly, the subcommittee believes it to be requisite to the use of arbitration as a means of enhancing internal government that fairly rigorous arbitral standards be established in those cases in which norms and procedures unique to higher education are implicated.

3. Selection and Education of Arbitrators

Much depends on the qualities of the individual selected to serve as the arbitrator and the degree to which he or she is educated by the parties to the issues for adjudication in the context of professional practice and custom and to the importance of the decision to the life of the institution. Here the Association can make a valuable contribution, whether or not a local affiliate is serving as a collective representative. As the preeminent organization of college and university faculty in the United States, the Association should share its expertise in reviewing the qualifications of proposed arbitrators and should consider, jointly with other organizations, consulting on the establishment of a national panel or regional panels of qualified individuals. Further, the Association may prepare model briefs or other materials dealing with accepted norms of academic practice to be used as educational materials before an arbitrator and should consider sponsoring, again possibly with other organizations, workshops for arbitrators on these issues. The Association should also maintain an up-to-date file of awards and provide detailed comments on their academic implications, perhaps in some published form. Since the use of arbitration in this setting is so novel, it is clear that for higher education, unlike for the industrial sector, no well-defined set of doctrines has been developed. It is incumbent on the Association to assist directly in shaping such doctrines through all available means. Toward this end the

[2]Regulation 15, "Recommended Institutional Regulations on Academic Freedom and Tenure," *Academe* 69 (January–February 1983): 20a.

[3]1958 "Statement on Procedural Standards in Faculty Dismissal Proceedings," *ibid.* 76 (May–June 1990): 42–44.

[4]Regulation 10, "Recommended Institutional Regulations," *op. cit.*, p. 19a.

[5]"Procedural Standards in the Renewal or Nonrenewal of Faculty Appointments," *Academe* 76 (January–February 1990): 48–51.

Association should establish a joint subcommittee of the national committees having an interest in this area. A detailed study of the actual effects of arbitration under the varying approaches currently practiced and the drafting of model arbitration clauses would fall within the purview of such a body.

Two final issues require attention: the rights of the individual under a collective agreement providing for arbitration as the terminal stage of the grievance procedure; and the Association's role in the event an arbitral award departs significantly from fundamental substantive standards sponsored by it.

Where there is an exclusive collective representative, the agent almost invariably controls access to arbitration. The subcommittee believes that this approach may be inappropriate in an academic setting and recommends that individual faculty members have access to arbitration on their own behalf if the collective representative refuses to press their claims. Because the issue placed before an arbitrator may touch deeply an individual's basic academic rights or freedoms, the individual should have the opportunity of participating in the selection of the arbitrator and have full rights to participate in all phases of the procedure, including all preliminaries, on a parity with the collective representative, if any, and the administration. Experimentation with the allocation of costs of proceedings where the representative does not itself desire to proceed to arbitration would be useful. Costs may be assessed by the arbitrator between the parties according to the gravity of the injury, if one is found, or could be borne equally by the administration and the complaining faculty member.

The Association has traditionally viewed itself as supporting basic standards and has not viewed its processes as being limited because of contrary provisions in an institution's regulations, or, for that matter, an adverse judicial determination. Equally, the Association should continue to challenge significant departures from elemental academic rights, whether or not these departures have warrant in a collective agreement or an arbitrator's award.

IV. SUMMARY

Arbitration can be a useful device for resolving some kinds of disputes and grievances that arise in academic life. Especially when collective bargaining is practiced, resort to arbitrators who are sensitive to the needs and standards of higher education may be the preferred way to avoid deadlocks or administrative domination. But arbitration is not a substitute for careful procedures that respect the autonomy of the faculty and administration in their respective spheres. A system of collective bargaining that routinely resorts to arbitration is an abdication of responsibility. This is especially true of the faculty's primary responsibility to determine who shall hold and retain faculty appointments.

Selected, Annotated Bibliography

Anderson, Paul J., and Goldstein, Rachael K. "Criteria of Journal Quality."
    Journal of Research Communication Studies, vol. 3 (1981), pp. 99–110.
Determines the frequency of faculty publications in eighty-eight primary biomedical journals and examines the characteristics of these journals to identify
possible criteria for journal quality. Comprehensive statements of editorial policies
and practices, descriptions of the referee system, explicit standards for manuscript
acceptance and rejection and frequency of citations of a journal by other journals
are proposed as tentative criteria for journal quality.

Bell, John G., and Seater, John J. "Publishing Performance: Departmental and
    Individual." *Economic Inquiry*, vol. 16 (1978), pp. 599–615.
Examines the publishing performance both of academic economics departments
and of individual academic economists. Introduces a new measure of performance and systematically compares and analyzes various measures of performance.
Compares department rankings produced by different methods and department
rankings over time. Also investigates the effect of tenure on individual performance.

Billings, Bradley B., and Viksnins, George J. "The Relative Quality of Economics
    Journals: An Alternative Ranking System." *Western Economic Journal*,
    vol. 10 (1972), pp. 467–69.
Criticizes William J. Moore's ranking of the fifty leading economics journals,
and proposes a rating scheme that is more powerful in distinguishing among
journals.

Braskamp, Larry A., Brandenburg, Dale C., and Ory, John C. *Evaluating Teach-
    ing Effectiveness: A Practical Guide*. Beverly Hills, California: Sage
    Publications, 1984.

Offers practical guidance to faculty and administrators in the critique, design and implementation of teaching evaluation. Takes a multiple purpose, criteria, and source approach consistent with current mainstream thinking and the AAUP position.

Brophy, Jere E. "Teacher Behavior and Its Effects." *Journal of Educational Psychology*, vol. 71 (1979), pp. 733–50.

Assesses present and possible future process-outcome research, emphasizing methodological considerations. Argues for compilation of detailed normative data about classrooms, including explication and integration of process-process as well as process-outcome relations. Suggests large, general field studies will give way to studies designed with particular contexts in mind, using appropriate measures of both processes and outcomes.

Bush, Winston C., Hamelman, Paul W., and Staaf, Robert J. "A Quality Index for Economic Journals." *Review of Economics and Statistics* (1974), pp. 123–25.

Uses the number of citations made to the articles published in an economic journal to construct an objective quality index for fourteen economic journals. Asserts that such an index is primarily a measure of the relative usefulness of the different journals as a research tool. Calculates a circulation per citation ratio to obtain a measure of journal productivity in terms of research.

Cartter, Allan M. *An Assessment of Quality in Graduate Education.* Washington, D.C.: American Council on Education, 1966.

Investigates the strengths and weaknesses of graduate schools in providing well-trained scholars for both teaching and research.

Cashin, William E. *IDEA Paper No. 20: Student Ratios of Teaching: A Summary of the Research.* Manhattan: Kansas State University, Center for Faculty Evaluation and Development, 1988.

Summarizes the conclusions of three major reviews of the student ratings literature. Offers broad, general conclusions. References all the major reviews of the ratings literature since 1970.

Cashin, William E., and Akihiro, Noma. *IDEA Technical Report No. 5: Description of IDEA Short Form Data Base.* Manhattan: Kansas State University, Center for Faculty Evaluation and Development, 1983.

Provides the rationale for the IDEA system in general and for the IDEA Short Form in particular. Also provides information about the development of the short form, the reports generated, and directions for administering the form.

Centra, John A. "Colleagues as Raters of Classroom Instruction." *Journal of Higher Education*, vol. 46 (1975), pp. 327–37.

Indicates that colleague rating of teaching effectiveness based primarily on classroom observation usually is not reliable enough to use in promotion and tenure discussions. Also discusses the aspects of teaching that colleagues typically are able to judge, along with other methods of assessing teaching.

Cole, Stephen, and Cole, Jonathan R. "Scientific Output and Recognition: A Study in the Operation of the Reward System in Science." *American Sociological Review* (1967), pp. 377–90.
Studies the relationship between quantity and quality of scientific output of 120 university physicists. An investigation of the community of physicists' response to patterns of research reveals that quality of output is more significant than quantity in eliciting professional recognition. Finds that the resultant reward system works to produce a higher correlation between quantity and quality of scientific output in top departments than in weaker ones.

Crane, Diana. "Scientists at Major and Minor Universities: A Study of Productivity and Recognition." *American Sociological Review* (1965), pp. 699–714.
Applies indices of productivity and recognition to the research careers of 150 scientists at three universities of varying prestige. Finds that graduates of major universities are more likely to be productive than those of minor ones and that attending a major graduate school has more effect on research productivity than current location at a major university.

Crooks, Terence J., and Kane, Michael T. "The Generalizability of Student Ratings of Instructors: Item Specificity and Section Effects." *Research in Higher Education*, vol. 15 (1981), pp. 305–13.
Examines the consistency of ratings between different sections of a course taught in a given semester by the same instructor, and compares the performance of global- and attribute-type instructor rating items. Finds that the section effect is small and that generalizability is substantially influenced by item specificity.

Dornbusch, Sanford M. "Perspectives from Sociology: Organizational Evaluation of Faculty Performances." *Academic Rewards in Higher Education*, ed. Darrell R. Lewis and William E. Becker, Jr. Cambridge, Massachusetts: Ballinger Publishing Company, 1979, pp. 41–60.
Uses an abstract theory of evaluation and authority to study faculty behavior at American colleges and universities. Investigates undergraduate teaching and research with respect to time spent on each, the influence of evaluations of each and the preferred influence of each at prestige, research and teaching institutions.

Feldman, Kenneth A. "The Superior College Teacher From the Students' View." *Research in Higher Education*, vol. 5 (1976), pp. 243–88.
Systematically analyzes the research on college students' views of the effectiveness of various instructor attitudes, behaviors, pedagogical practices to identify characteristics consistently associated with superior college teaching. Concludes with interpretations and cautions.

Gilmore, Gerald M., Kane, Michael T., and Naccareto, Richard W. "The Generalizability of Student Ratings of Instruction: Estimation of the Teacher and Course Components." *Journal of Educational Measurement*, vol. 15 (1978), pp. 1–13.
Reports the results of two studies that isolate teacher and course effects. In one

study, course effects were tested within teacher effects; in the other, teacher effects were tested within course effects. The teacher-course interaction variance is estimated indirectly by combining the results of the two studies.

Graves, Philip E., Marchand, James R., and Thompson, Randall. "Economics Department Rankings; Research Incentives, Constraints, and Efficiency." *American Economic Review*, vol. 72 (1982), pp. 1131–41.
Ranks economics departments on the basis of page counts of articles published in twenty-four top journals, and establishes new methodological and empirical approaches to school quality assessment. In addition to page counts, departments were surveyed regarding teaching load, teaching and research assistance, secretarial resources and student faculty ratios, thus facilitating insights on relative, as well as absolute, departmental quality.

Hagstrom, Warren O. "Input, Outputs, and the Prestige of University Science Department." *Sociology of Education*, vol. 44 (1971), pp. 375–97.
Reports correlates of departmental prestige for a sample of 125 departments in mathematics, physics, chemistry and biology. Uses multivariate linear regression. Large and significant correlations with departmental prestige are found to exist for measures of department size, research production, research opportunities, faculty background, student characteristics and faculty awards and offices.

Hawkins, Robert G., Ritter, Lawrence S., and Ingo, Walter. "What Economists Think of Their Journals." *Journal of Political Economy*, vol. 81 (1973), pp. 1017–32.
Seeks to identify the economics profession's perceptions of its media as well as the apparent differences of views regarding media prestige existing in a number of subgroups among economists. Finds that it is the quality of output that counts, not where or how it is published, in evaluating the output of economists, but that there is also a pervasive tendency to give weight to the journal in which a person's work appears.

Hildebrand, Milton. "The Character and Skills of the Excellent Professor." *Journal of Higher Education*, vol. 4 (1973), pp. 41–51.
Emphasizes the results of his former study that contribute to the characterization of effective teaching. Identifies five distinct components of effective teaching. Asserts that teachers who are regarded as strong in all five areas are considered to be excellent by students and faculty alike.

Hogan, Timothy D. "Rankings of Ph.D. Programs in Economics and the Relative Publishing Performance of Their Ph.D.'s: The Experience of the 1960's." *Western Economic Journal*, vol. 11 (1973), pp. 429–50.
Analyzes the publishing performance of economists with respect to the institutions at which they received their graduate training. Finds that a very high proportion of the total pages in highly ranked economics journals have been written by Ph.D.s from a small number of graduate programs.

House, Donald R., and Yaeger, James H. "The Distribution of Publications Success Within and Among Top Economics Departments: A Disaggregative View of Recent Evidence." *Economic Inquiry*, vol. 16 (1978), pp. 599–615.
Offers a more detailed approach to the analysis of journal output by determining the distribution of research skills within departments. Develops and obtains various measures of publication success among faculty members within each professorial rank, so that the research output of these ranks can be compared within and across departments.

Irby, D. M. "Clinical Faculty Development." *Clinical Education for the Allied Health Professions*, ed. C. Ford. St. Louis: C. B. Mosby Company, 1978, pp. 95–110.
Assists allied health educators in planning, developing, and evaluating clinical education programs. Although the book focuses on the issues of clinical education, it is in the context of total (clinical plus academic) program improvement.

Issler, Klaus. "A Conception of Excellence in Teaching." *Education*, vol. 1031 (1983), pp. 338–43.
Offers an alternative to the process-product conception of teaching as the basis for an inquiry into teaching excellence. Also identifies eleven factors which are essential for teaching excellence.

Jauch, Lawrence R., and Glueck, William F. "Evaluation of University Professors' Research Performance." *Management Sciences*, vol. 22 (1975), pp. 66–75.
Systematically compares multiple measures of research output to identify those which are effective for the evaluation of research professors. Finds that a simple count of the number of publications in respectable journals is an effective measure of performance.

Kasten, Katherine Lewellan. "Tenure and Merit Pay as Rewards for Research, Teaching, and Service at a Research University." *Journal of Higher Education*, vol. 44 (1984), pp. 500–14.
Examines the values faculty place on research, teaching and service when conferring tenure and merit pay. Finds that faculty work in research is tightly coupled to faculty rewards. Also finds that teaching and service have significant effects on the allocation of rewards, but these effects are moderate and somewhat idiosyncratic.

Katz, David A. "Faculty Salaries, Promotions, and Productivity at a Large University." *American Economic Review* (1973), pp. 469–77.
Uses data from a large, highly ranked public university to intensively study the determinants of faculty salaries and promotions. Demonstrates the feasibility of quantifying many of the important determinants of faculty salaries and promotions.

Kulik, James A., and McKeachie, Wilbert J. "The Evaluation of Teachers in

Higher Education." *Review of Research in Higher Education*, ed. Fred N. Kerlinger. Itasca, Illinois: F. E. Peacock Publishers, Inc., 1975, pp. 210–40.
Considers two kinds of procedures for evaluating teachers. Examines student ratings plus other evaluations requiring observer inference. Concludes with an examination of direct measurement of student performance.

Leland, David N. "Article Popularity." *Economic Inquiry*, vol. 24 (1986), pp. 113–80.
Examines the causes and consequences of article popularity, and finds that author reputation, article length and journal quality are strong determinants of article popularity.

Liebowitz, S. J., and Palmer, J. P. "Assessing the Relative Impacts of Economics Journals." *Journal of Economic Literature*, vol. 22 (1984), pp. 77–88.
Provides a ranking of journals based on their relative influences on the writing of academics. Uses the number of citations that authors make to articles to create this ranking.

Lin, Yi-Guang, McKeachie, W. J., and Tucker, David G. "The Use of Student Ratings in Promotion Decisions." *Journal of Higher Education*, vol. 55 (1984), pp. 583–89.
Tests the effects on promotion decisions of two different methods of presenting data from student evaluations. This study derives from theories of influence developed in social psychology and communications. Finds that a combination of statistical summaries of student ratings and direct quotations from students is more effective than statistical evidence alone.

Manis, Jerome G. "Some Academic Influences Upon Publication Productivity." *Social Forces*, vol. 29 (1951), pp. 267–72.
Describes an attempt to analyze certain aspects of the social scientist's publication activity. The chief aspect investigated is that of certain factors influencing publishing productivity. Underscores the multifariousness of the conditions influencing academic output.

Marsh, Herbert W. "Student Evaluations of University Teaching: Research Findings, Methodological Issues, and Directions for Future Research." *International Journal of Educational Research*, vol. 11 (1987), pp. 253–388.
Provides an overview of findings and the methods used to study students' evaluations of teaching effectiveness. Summarizes the author's own research and a wide range of other research.

Meltzer, Bernard N. "The Productivity of Social Scientists." *American Journal of Sociology* (July 1949), pp. 25–29.
Attempts to isolate predictive correlates of the publishing of articles and books by social scientists. Inquires into the relationship between the quantity and quality of publication and various educational factors. Finds rate of educational progress

and early publishing to have significant association with quantity of publication. Finds similarly for the quality of publication.

Moore, William J. "The Relative Quality of Economics Journals." *Western Economic Journal* (1972), pp. 156–69.
Suggests a formal rating system for estimating the quality of economics journals, and uses it to rate fifty leading economics journals. The proposed system is built upon the assumption that the quality of a journal is closely related to the overall professional accomplishments of its contributors and that such accomplishments, in turn, are closely related to the quality of the contributors' institutional affiliations.

Murray, Harry G. *Evaluating University Teaching: A Review of Research.* Toronto: Ontario Confederation of University Association, 1980.
Reviews the research on the evaluation of college teaching since the 1973 OCUFA publication. Focuses on student evaluation of teaching, but not to the exclusion of other evaluation methods.

Overall, J. U., and Marsh, Herbert W. "Students' Evaluation of Instruction: A Longitudinal Study of Their Stability." *Journal of Educational Psychology*, vol. 72 (1980), pp. 321–25.
Investigates the long-term stability of students' evaluation of instructional effectiveness. Results show large and statistically significant correlations between end-of-term and retrospective ratings.

Roose, Kenneth D., and Anderson, Charles J. *A Rating of Graduate Programs.* Washington, D.C.: American Council on Education, 1970.
Presents the principal findings of the 1969 Survey of Graduate Education. Appraises faculties and programs on the basis of their reputations. Also comments on the implications for institutional policies.

Rugg, Edwin A., and Norris, Raymond C. "Student Ratings of Individualized Faculty Supervision: Description and Evaluation." *American Educational Research Journal*, vol. 12 (1975), pp. 41–53.
Describes and evaluates faculty supervision in individualized, research-oriented learning experiences. A principle axes analysis of student responses yields 10 first-order and 2 second-order factors which focus on descriptive aspects of the supervision, plus 2 first-order factors which refer to aspects of student satisfaction with experience and supervision.

Seldin, Peter. *Changing Practices in Faculty Evaluation.* San Francisco: Jossey-Bass, 1984.
Distills the literature on successful evaluation programs, revealing changes and trends in policies and practices for assessing faculty performance. Studies the transformation of faculty evaluation programs over time and identifies implications for the future.

——. *Successful Faculty Evaluation Programs.* Crugers, New York: Coventry Press, 1980.

Designed to help professors and administrators avoid the pitfalls and develop the requisite skills and sensitivity for a successful evaluation program. Discusses seven separate areas of faculty evaluation: student colleague and self-assessment, student learning, student advising, institutional service and research and publication. Provides practical strategies, sample appraisal forms and specific guidelines.

Sherman, Thomas M. *et al.* "The Quest for Excellence in University Teaching." *Journal of Higher Education*, vol. 481 (1987), pp. 67–83.
Examines the literature on college teaching and instructional design to generate a conception of teaching excellence in higher education. Finds that there are qualities and conditions that separate excellent teachers from those who are very good, competent and incompetent.

Siegfried, John J. "The Publishing of Economic Papers and Its Impact on Graduate Faculty Ratings, 1960–1969." *Journal of Economic Literature*, vol. 10 (1972), pp. 31–49.
Updates prior tabulations of publishing performance by institutional affiliation of authors of economic papers, tabulates similar information for additional journals, examines the data for biases and explores the relationship between faculty quality and publishing quantity.

Siegfried, John J., and White, Kenneth J. "Teaching and Publishing as Determinants of Academic Salaries." *Journal of Economic Education* (1973), pp. 90–98.
Examines the faculty reward structure in the economics department at a large public university in order to identify the relative rewards for teaching and research activities. The analysis suggests that while teaching is rewarded, research output and administrative experience are the predominant determinants of faculty salary levels.

Skeels, Jack W., and Taylor, Ryland A. "The Relative Quality of Economics Journals: An Alternative Rating System." *Western Economic Journal* (1972), pp. 470–73.
Constructs a quality index for economics journals with the assumption that the quality of a journal is judged by the quality of its contents. The index proposed is built upon lists of quality articles, the sources of which are reading lists for various disciplines within economics.

Slaughter, Sheila, and Silva, Edward T. "Service and the Dynamics of Developing Fields." *Journal of Higher Education*, vol. 54 (1983), pp. 481–99.
Compares higher education's contemporary emergence as a scholarly specialty with the turn-of-the-century development of some of the specialties that currently supply higher education's conceptual apparatus. Notes parallels between these emerging social sciences at the turn of the century and today's higher education.

Smith, Richard, and Fiedler, Fred E. "The Measurement of Scholarly Work: A Critical Review of the Literature." *Educational Record* (Summer 1971), pp. 225–32.

Critically compares various measures of scholarly output, and finds that the citation measure is least contaminated by prestige factors or publication volume. Also concludes that no currently available measure is sufficiently well established to stand alone.

Sprinthall, Normal A., and Thies-Sprinthall, Lois. "The Teacher As an Adult Learner: A Cognitive-Developmental View." *Staff Development Part II*, ed. Gary A. Griffin. Chicago, Illinois: University of Chicago Press, 1983.
Outlines a series of theoretical advances that may form a theoretical basis for addressing the problem of teacher development from the perspective of the teacher as an adult learner. Also reviews previous conceptual frameworks of teacher development plus both the theory and evidence supporting the importance of a cognitive-developmental perspective.

Stigler, George J., and Friedland, Clare. "The Citation Practices of Doctorates in Economics." *Journal of Political Economy*, vol. 83 (1975), pp. 477–507.
Analyzes the citations of doctorates in economics from six major universities for the period from 1950 to 1968 in two fields of value theory. Examines the citations for commonality in the use of authorities and for parochialism. The citation practices of the authorities are also examined compared with those of the doctorates, and used to define scientific associates and adversaries.

Tuckman, Howard P. *Publication, Teaching, and the Academic Reward Structure.* Lexington, Massachusetts: Lexington Books, 1976.
Explores the nature of the reward structure of American universities. Analyzes the nature of the market for academic labor and empirically investigates the reward structure in several different disciplines found at the modern university. Ultimately develops a conceptual and empirical perspective on the academic reward structure.

Tuckman, Howard P., Gapinski, James H., and Hagemann, Robert P. "Faculty Skills and the Salary Structure in Academe: A Market Perspective." *American Economic Review*, vol. 67 (1977), pp. 692–702.
Investigates the determinants of faculty salary using a comprehensive data set. Hypothesizes a relationship between salaries and market evaluation of skills. Finds that publishing and administration carry much larger returns than teaching and public service and that women earn less than men with like characteristics.

Tuckman, Howard P., and Hagemann, Robert P. "An Analysis of the Reward Structure in Two Disciplines." *Journal of Higher Education*, vol. 47 (1976), pp. 447–64.
Uses regression analysis to estimate the relative absolute return to particular skills of full-time male faculty at American universities in two fields: economics and education. Also gives a method for qualifying the lifetime returns to publication. Finds publishers are more highly rewarded than their unpublished colleagues in both disciplines, while outstanding teaching does not appear to be rewarded in either field.

Weaver, Frederick S. "Scholarship and Teaching." *Education Record*, vol. 70
      (1989), pp. 54–58.
Argues that there are substantial complementarities between good teaching
and faculty scholarship, despite the assertion of recent reports that scholarly
engagement and teaching are essentially independent, competing phenomena.
Contends that this assertion is based on two serious misconceptions, resulting in
a distorted understanding about the relationship between teaching and scholarship. Submits that teaching faculty's continuing intellectual vitality and development necessitate a continuing program of writing and publication.

Index

About the Authors

DAVID A. DILTS is Professor of Economics and Labor Relations at Indiana University-Purdue University at Fort Wayne. He has coauthored six books on labor relations including *Labor Relations Law in State and Local Government* (Quorum, 1992).

LAWRENCE J. HABER is Associate Professor of Economics at Indiana University-Purdue University at Fort Wayne. He has published widely in the journal literature on his major field of interest, economic theory.

DONNA BIALIK is Assistant Professor of Economics at Indiana University-Purdue University at Fort Wayne.